C000225131

Getting on Better with Teenagers

A companion website to accompany this book is available online at:
http://education.dixie2.continuumbooks.com
    Please type in the URL above and receive your unique password for access
to the book's online resources.
    If you experience any problems accessing the resources, please contact
Continuum at: info@continuumbooks.com

Also by Gererd Dixie

Managing Your Classroom, second edition
Trainee Primary Teacher's Handbook
Trainee Secondary Teacher's Handbook
The Ultimate Teaching Manual

Getting on Better with Teenagers

Improving Behaviour and Learning through Positive Relationships

Gererd Dixie

continuum

The Continuum International Publishing Group

The Tower Building	80 Maiden Lane
11 York Road	Suite 704
London SE1 7NX	New York NY 10038

www.continuumbooks.com

© Gererd Dixie 2011

All rights reserved. No part of this publication may be reproduced or transmitted in any form or by any means, electronic or mechanical, including photocopying, recording, or any information storage or retrieval system, without prior permission in writing from the publishers.

Gererd Dixie has asserted his right under the Copyright, Designs and Patents Act, 1988, to be identified as Author of this work.

British Library Cataloguing-in-Publication Data
A catalogue record for this book is available from the British Library.

ISBN: 978-1-4411-5923-6 (paperback)
       978-1-4411-9847-1 (hardcover)

Library of Congress Cataloging-in-Publication Data
Dixie, Gererd.
    Getting on Better with Teenagers : Improving Behaviour and Learning
    Through Positive Relationships / Gererd Dixie.
        p. cm.
        Includes index.
        ISBN 978-1-4411-5923-6 – ISBN 978-1-4411-9847-1 – ISBN 978-1-4411-1432-7 –
ISBN 978-1-4411-4466-9 1. Teacher-student relationships. 2. Teenagers and adults.
3. Effective teaching. I. Title.

    LB1033.D565 2011
    373.1102'3--dc22

                                                                2011011506

Typeset by Newgen Imaging Systems Pvt Ltd, Chennai, India
Printed and bound in India

Contents

Introduction

Before you start flicking through these pages to check out whether you think it's worth reading this book, I feel I need to convey this important message. As a teacher with over thirty years' experience, I fully understand the rigours and stresses of the job. Sometimes there are so many demands placed upon you that you simply do not know which way to turn. Sometimes you are so tired that you do not have the capacity to think. The last thing that a busy and stressed teacher needs is to have to wade through pages and pages of theoretical jargon about what he, or she, should be doing in the classroom.

This book, therefore, has been written with real teenagers, real teachers and realistic classroom scenarios in mind. Although the book may have an academic flavour in places, it has been written primarily as a down-to-earth practical guide to establishing, maintaining and developing good working relationships with your students. Having said this, I am going to break my rule just this once, and describe to you in detail a piece of academic research that has done more to shape my teaching career than anything else. This work is *Adapting Supervisory Practices to Different Orientations of Teaching Competence* by American educational researchers Zimpher and Howey (1987). I am sure that you will note the 'dated' nature of this source with some surprise, and you are absolutely right to do so. However, in all my experience as a teacher and learner, I have not come across a more relevant or apposite piece of work when it comes to classifying teacher roles. This article has become my bible and has served to inform my own teaching as well as the training I have offered to 'beginning' teachers throughout my career. The relevance and context of this research will be revealed to you as you make your journey through the book.

Zimpher and Howey describe the four types of teacher competence which they believe to be critical to effective teaching and which I feel all teachers should know about. These four are technical competence, clinical competence, critical competence and personal competence. The details of each of these are outlined below:

Teachers display *technical competence* when they:

- determine *what* is to be learned;
- determine *how* it is to be learned;
- employ the criteria by which success is to be measured;
- show mastery of methods of instruction, for example, specific skills such as how to ask good questions;
- apply appropriate teaching strategies;
- select and organize appropriate resources;
- structure the classroom for learning;
- employ techniques that are successful in helping to establish and maintain good classroom discipline.

So, what does this mean in practical terms? How does a teacher's deployment of the technical domain manifest itself in the classroom? With these questions in mind I have furnished you with a number of school-based scenarios where teachers use their technical competence. You will be able to demonstrate your technical competence by:

- using the 'tricks of the trade' in order to gain class control (setting up expectations, rules, routines, rewards, sanctions, scanning, seating plans, tactical pausing, choice direction, and proximity praise);
- organizing the classroom and resources in such a way as to maximize learning time; this could mean having resources already laid out on the desks for pupils to pick up when they enter the room.
- adopting strategies designed to avoid the marginalization of students; this means making sure that every pupil makes a verbal contribution during lessons.

Teachers display *clinical competence* when they:

- adopt the role of a problem solver and clinician who is able to frame and solve practical problems through the process of reflective action and inquiry;
- set up and test hypotheses in the classroom, and solve such problems as what should be done about disruptive student behaviour, or what the best format for group work should be;
- take on the role of action researcher, exploring the extent to which the various learning theories match the realities of classroom life.

You can display your clinical competence in your practice by:

- demonstrating an ability to 'reflect-in-action' (as you teach) and 'reflect-on-action' (after the lesson has taken place) and showing a willingness to identify implications for your future practice and to implement your newly gained knowledge and understanding in your practice;
- being able to solve professional and pedagogic problems through the collaborative process; you can do this by working with your Head of Year (HOY) to support challenging students or by working with your Special Educational Needs Co-ordinator (SENCO) to find ways to support the low-ability students in your lessons;
- being willing to experiment with different learning styles/scenarios and by evaluating your practice; you can do this by finding out about pupils' dominant learning styles and using this information to plan your lessons.

Teachers display *critical competence* when they:

- adopt a critical role of the education system by exploring such issues as the social conditions of schooling, and the influence of the 'hidden curriculum';
- explore the power and authority bases both within and outside the school;
- ask questions about the basic ideology of schools, about the nature of society in general, and about the effects of negative socialization on the teaching process;

- ask other questions that present a more critical and radical notion of the structures of schools.

So again, what does this mean in practice? You will be able to display your critical competence by:

- showing how you use the hidden curriculum in the learning process by recognizing that a great deal of student learning occurs subliminally through messages conveyed in display material, in resources chosen and in interactions between teachers and students. You can show this understanding by planning classroom displays that demonstrate the qualities, skills, knowledge and understanding required by young people as they move into the adult world;

- using your understanding of learning theory to support your teaching and students' learning. Your knowledge of learning theory will be seen in your choice of behaviour management and learning strategies. For example, will you adopt a behaviourist approach or a humanist approach to classroom management or will you use a combination of both approaches?

- showing an understanding of wider educational initiatives/issues and how these affect your role in the classroom. You can do this by exploring such initiatives as Every Child Matters and applying them to your everyday practice;

- having an understanding of how societal factors affect students' learning – unemployment, housing, attitudes towards education. Use this knowledge to inform your interactions with, and expectations of, your students. Although you cannot realistically expect to influence the things that affect the students outside school, showing empathy for their situations can have a very positive impact on your relationships with them in the classroom.

Teachers display *personal* competence when they:

- use themselves as effective and humane instruments of classroom instruction;
- use their intra-personal skills to critically confront themselves and develop their levels of self-awareness;
- fully understand the interactive nature of teaching by showing an awareness of the role of verbal and non-verbal symbols in the teaching process;

- understand how small group processes work;
- use their good interpersonal skills to create a warm and supportive learning environment.

Again, it is important to translate the theoretical descriptions offered above into tangible examples of classroom practice. You will be able to display your personal competence by:

- demonstrating good professional relationships with your students, colleagues and parents; you can do this by remaining as objective about emotive issues and by not gossiping or denigrating pupils or staff;
- displaying empathy, humour and teacher warmth; even when admonishing students it is important to do so within a warm affirming framework, making sure that they know that you are unhappy with their behaviour and not with them as individuals;
- offering students strong moral guidance through stories and personal anecdotes, and by modelling this in your personal behaviour; where possible and appropriate, use your experiences in lessons to demonstrate that we all make mistakes and that nobody is too old to learn;
- displaying a passion for your subject and/or from teaching in general. Don't hold back from using animated body language and tone of voice or for demonstrating excitement and wonder about the topics you are teaching; pupils may be superficially cynical about this, but deep down they prefer their teachers to believe in what they are teaching;
- displaying assertive and positive body language and by dominating your teaching space; it is absolutely vital that your pupils have confidence in you as their teacher – even if you are not totally confident about a topic or about teaching a particular class, don't show it;
- creating a 'can do' culture in your teaching/learning space. Always be positive towards your students. Find out and celebrate what they can do and do not over-focus on their weaknesses.

All of these competences are important, but if you aspire to be a highly successful teacher, you need to make sure that you are not over-reliant on one particular domain. You need, therefore, to adopt a considered and balanced approach towards your teaching role. Although most students are not fully able to articulate the prerequisites for being a good teacher, I am convinced that they do ask a number of quite searching internal questions about the person standing in front of them. My research into student–teacher relationships, together with my lengthy teaching experience, has shown me that students *do* see good teachers as being able to control their classes and make their teaching spaces purposeful and create effective scenarios for learning. They *really do* want their teachers to reflect on the things that work and don't work in the classroom; they *do* want the teacher to understand how their home backgrounds and family situations affect their work in school.

The other really important point for me to make here is that these four competences do not exist in isolation. A teacher has many roles in school, and it is virtually impossible to place these domains into discrete categories. Although I am aware that these roles overlap, and that they are equally important in their own right, for the purpose of this book, I focus mainly on the personal, clinical and technical competences. It is predominantly these that contribute to the making of teachers who are able to build good working relationships with their students. Surely this has got to be the principle aim of any successful teacher. Without such relationships effective learning will simply not take place. This book recognizes the importance of establishing successful teacher–student partnerships, and offers guidance and advice as to how this partnership can be fully realized.

Who is the book for and why has it been written?

As a Professional Development Tutor, I have made numerous Local authority and school-based presentations to Initial Teacher Training (ITT) students, newly qualified teachers (NQTs) and teachers who are still in the dawn of their careers. I call this group of teachers 'beginning' teachers. Feedback from these sessions, as well as from numerous individual mentoring sessions with these teachers, has shown me quite clearly the need for a book such as this. These teachers want to know why they are experiencing behavioural, learning and relational problems with specific youngsters in their classes, when the very same students seem to be able to strike up good working relationships with other teachers in the school. It is a source of great frustration to them that, no matter what they do to try to redress these issues, their relationships with these students don't seem to get any better.

So, why is this book necessary? The interactive nature of teaching means that the establishment and maintenance of good working relationships with students are at the heart of good discipline and effective learning. The strategies required for teachers to gain effective classroom control are often covered in depth in post-graduate certificate in education (PGCE) courses. Monitoring and assessment issues are also given a great deal of attention. Any weaknesses in subject knowledge can be compensated for by teachers' carrying out individual research and/or through their experiences of having to teach unfamiliar units of work. However, the issue of teacher–student relationships is often not given the focus it deserves. Although there seems to be a substantial amount of literature that deals with whole-class behavioural issues, I am convinced that there is a need for a book that focuses on the importance of teacher–student relationships in the learning equation. It is my belief that good teacher–student relationships are at the very heart of quality learning. Although this book has been written primarily with 'beginning teachers' in mind, I feel confident that it will benefit any practising teacher, irrespective of their age or position on the career ladder. I also believe that this publication should be on the shelves of all professional development tutors, who will be able to use the mass of realistic exemplar scenarios and exercises for their school-based in-service sessions.

What is in this book?

This book is divided into six chapters, each one focusing on a distinct area relevant to the core issue, that of establishing, maintaining and developing positive learning relationships between teachers and students.

Through the medium of free-response questionnaires, the initial chapter briefly explores a number of adults' memories of teachers. The purpose of this chapter is to raise the reader's awareness of the impact that teachers can have on our lives, right through into adult life. Through a discussion of the various traits and characteristics of effective teachers, this chapter offers the reader some excellent role models of good teaching. The latter part of the chapter describes some of the bad memories respondents have had of their teachers and then goes on to explore the effects that these have in their later lives.

Bearing in mind that teaching is very much a 'two-way' process and that real learning depends largely upon successful student–teacher relationships, it is very important for teachers to reflect constructively on their practice. Chapter Two asks the question: 'What kind of teacher are you?' Through the use of a Teaching-Styles audit, readers will be given the opportunity to analyze and evaluate their own traits and characteristics, and to explore the effects that these may have on their relationships with the students in their classes.

The initial part of Chapter Three looks briefly at the marketization of education, and focuses on the need for teachers to gain an understanding of their students' perceptions of their teaching. The chapter goes on to offer some research findings that describe a range of student perceptions of their teachers, before then exploring the possible implications for your teaching.

Chapter Four shows how being a good classroom leader and creating a positive classroom climate can really enhance the quality of teacher–student relationships and, as a result, improve learning scenarios in school. Much of the advice and guidance offered within this chapter will be presented through an exploration of 'brain-based learning'.

Much has been said in the media in recent years about the poor behaviour of some students in schools. Chapter Five describes some of the characteristics of this antisocial behaviour before going on to explore a number of possible reasons behind the actions of disaffected students. The chapter builds on the previous one by offering strategies and guidance designed to build good working relationships with those disaffected students for whom whole-class management strategies have failed.

Perhaps the most demanding role for all practising teachers is that of being a form tutor. Chapter Six offers advice and guidance on how to be a successful, effective and popular form tutor. The chapter describes ways in which teachers can provide formal and informal opportunities for the personal and social development of their students. It then goes on to suggest how to create an infrastructure that will support the school's ethos on behaviour and attitudes. The chapter concludes by exploring the way in which teachers can support the academic progress of their students, and also act as an efficient conduit for communications between school and home.

How to use this book

You might like to read this book from cover to cover in order to get an over-all picture of the themes, issues and recommended practices explored in each chapter. Each chapter stands on its own so, alternatively, you may wish to turn to a specific chapter to explore a particular issue that is relevant to your needs. Finally, it is important for me to make it clear that references to individual teachers and situations made in this book have been changed in order to ensure that anonymity has been maintained.

Wherever you see this symbol, go to the companion website to find downloadable resources for you to use in class.

1   No one forgets a good teacher

Between the years 2000 and 2001, the Teacher Training and Development Agency for Schools ran an inspirational campaign entitled, No One Forgets a Good Teacher! This recruiting message was shown extensively on cinema and television screens and on billboards across the country, and it inspired me, and thousands like me, to think about my own recollections of teachers. The fundamental question we all were asking at times was, what were the magic ingredients that brought these teachers so fondly to the forefront of our thoughts? This chapter will provide you with some of the answers.

Whenever I delve back into the distant past and begin to reminisce about my school days, I do not immediately recall the subject matter we covered in lessons. My mind doesn't start to dwell on questions such as who won the Battle of Waterloo, what exactly Pythagoras had to offer, or why the flood plains of rivers are so important. As important as all these topics are, they certainly did not provide a major focus for my memories. Instead, I start to reminisce about *the way* I was taught and about the teachers who took the time and trouble to really get to know me. I think fondly of those teachers who managed to inspire me, to make me laugh, to make me think, and, above all, to make me care about myself and about the world in which we live. Unfortunately for me, my experiences with these teachers were few and far between. My memories of my school days are at best clouded and, at worst, unhappy. It is fair to say therefore, that my academic, social and emotional development took place long after I left school. Any success I have had in life is down to a combination of latent ability, being in the right place at the right time, plenty of encouragement from those dear to me and a great deal of self-motivation and determination. How I wish that my teachers had read the following job description, taken from the prospectus of a leading teacher-training university:

A good teacher is:

- energetic;
- a good communicator;
- able to inspire and enthuse;
- enjoys working with young people;
- a good manager of resources, material and time;
- imaginative and creative and has a sense of humour!

> Teaching is a demanding career, physically, emotionally and intellectually. It calls for energy, dedication, patience and enthusiasm. You must have enthusiasm for your subject, and, far more important, you must be able to form a relationship with and control the class. Class management skills are essential. You also need to be able to think on your feet. This is not a nine-to-five job. There will be a lot of preparation and marking to do in the evenings and week-ends. There are also exams to prepare, invigilate and mark. All this calls for good time management, self-discipline, administration and organizational skills as well as good supervisory and leadership skills.

Or you may want to consider looking at this guidance information published by a teacher employment agency, which offered this pithy job description of the requirements of a good teacher.

What skills and abilities do I need?

> It sounds basic but it is essential you like and relate well to kids! A good teacher will be committed to opening up young minds. You'll also need excellent communication skills, a keen intellect, creativity and bags of energy. It also helps to have a sense of humour.

Let's face it, if you were taught by teachers who met all of these criteria you would most certainly remember them, wouldn't you? Just think of the impact these teachers would have made in terms of increasing your motivation levels and in providing you with the knowledge, skills, values and attitudes you need to live a successful and happy life.

I have briefly described some of the experiences of my own school days to you, but what I want to do is to also furnish you with a number of memories different adults have of their teachers. In order to gain these, I issued questionnaires to the 170 members of the teaching and non-teaching staff in two secondary schools. The research brief was simple. I wanted them to recount their memories of their primary and/or secondary school teachers. The response was simply overwhelming, both in terms of the written replies that I received and in the amount of discussion and experience sharing the process initiated. It was obvious that in asking this question, I had really hit a nerve! I couldn't walk down the corridor without someone wanting to talk to me about their early school experiences. So, why have I included the results of this research in this book? What is the relevance of these findings to the core purpose of this publication? The answer is simple. I feel that there is much to be learned from the reflections of adults on their childhood days in schools, especially if those adults are teachers! What became absolutely apparent at a very early stage in this research was how important teachers are in the formative stages of our lives. It is important that you, as 'beginning teachers', cast your minds back to your own school days. Think about the characteristics of the teachers who inspired you, and of those who lacked the ability to motivate you. You will be able to use these memories to good effect when building relationships with your own students. However, let me get one thing straight. I am not suggesting that teachers simply become 'carbon copies' of their heroes – that would be both inappropriate and unrealistic. However, I do feel that, on our journey through life, we both consciously and unconsciously select, and take on, many of the characteristics of the people we admire, and that these gradually become subsumed into our personality. Providing a teacher recreates these characteristics in one's own style, I see nothing wrong with this. What is important for you as beginning teachers to note, however, is that you need to become your own person as soon as possible – students will respect you for it.

I found it fascinating to read through the results of this low-level primary research. Processing this material, however, was quite difficult. Because of the 'emotional' nature of this issue and, because I wanted to obtain a high degree of validity in my findings, I used a free-response style questionnaire to elicit the thoughts, feelings and emotions that surfaced in people's minds when asked to think about their teachers. Although the results were highly relevant and useful, many of the responses were free-flowing andsomewhat lacking in focus. They were, therefore, quite difficult to categorize. As you will see below, I have used three broad categories to describe the experiences of the research population.

Motivation, enthusiasm, interest in the individual and encouragement

In virtually all the responses made by the sample research population, there was some reference made to the teacher's enthusiasm for their subject, their encouragement of and interest in the individual, and their sheer passion for teaching. To capture the flavour of my findings I have included a number of extracts from their responses below.

I remember him because of his sheer enthusiasm for everything he did. Obviously he was heavily involved in school sports and he was very encouraging towards me.

My favourite teacher showed enthusiasm and a love of their subject – you aspired to be like them.

Mr X opened my eyes to Media Studies and I have always said that it is down to him that I now teach this subject. He had a passion for media, and most of the information he gave us had come from his own research, not textbooks, and I really admired him for that. He opened my eyes to new films and ideas, which I surprised myself by liking them . . . I remember him today mostly because when I plan for lessons for new topics I always think about how he'd do it. If I can imagine him teaching my lesson, I know it's right.

Geography was never really a subject that I would have said that I actually 'enjoyed' until I had this teacher. As a result of his lessons my perception was altered and I went on to do Geography A Level. (The subject I got my best A Level grade in!) I always knew how hard the teacher worked for us and in return I always ensured I worked equally hard. The teacher's enthusiasm for the subject really inspired me and made me want to learn . . . this is the teacher that made me want to enter the profession – I hope that I am able to inspire students in the same way.

Mr X was my history teacher for GCSE and A level. He was enthusiastic and knew a lot of stuff! He made the subject relevant and exciting to study . . . He made me see that history is the most important subject in the world – to understand human nature, decisions, events and to make sense of the world in which we live. He inspired me to learn and to become a teacher.

My favourite teacher at secondary school was Mrs X who taught me English . . . the interest and enthusiasm she exuded prompted my enthusiasm and when I pondered on becoming an English teacher, I thought of her." She was my Maths teacher in Year 10 – enthusiastic and positive and always made me feel good about myself. I was in the top group for Maths but I never felt confident until she began to teach me . . . Unfortunately I changed teacher the next year and my performance went downhill.

My geography teacher motivated me so much I thought about being a geography teacher – that is until I had a different A Level teacher.

I was not good at sport. Mr X introduced rugby to the school so I was at the same level as everybody else. I played for the school and the Norwich team. He again made me feel I could do it. The other PE teachers would coach the best students during lessons leaving the rest of us kick about at the bottom of the field. Without Mr X I would have remained a school refuser. Why do I remember him? He was kind and was interested in what I could do.

I went to a secondary modern school. My headteacher, Mr X, proved that we weren't failures simply because we were not at the grammar school. He fought to enable us to take O' Levels and not just CSEs. He timetabled a range of subjects, e.g., army corps, car maintenance, farming, office work as well as pushing the more able students to achieve academically. Back in 1967 he encouraged me to take O Level maths in Year 4 (10). He later fought for us to do A Levels at our school.

My music teacher changed my life! He spotted my potential straight away. Until then I had been rather average. He encouraged me, made me believe in myself and then there was no stopping me . . . .

So, what can we learn from these memories? The one dominant theme to evolve from these research findings is that adults remember good teachers for their passion and enthusiasm for teaching. In my role as Professional Development Tutor, I observed hundreds of lessons. There is, however, one which I remember above all others. I was observing a trainee science teacher delivering a lesson on electricity that involved him explaining to the students how to read electric meters. The lesson started brightly enough with the trainee launching the lesson in a reasonably assertive manner. However, as the lesson continued I saw his facial expression, tone of voice and general body language change quite dramatically. The blood drained from the poor fellow's face, and it got to the point where he was even failing to make eye contact with the students while he was explaining the work. You can imagine the impact this had on the behaviour of the students in the class – the youngsters began to lose focus and started to chat to each other, leaving the poor trainee standing at the front of the room talking to himself. In our post-observation discussion I suggested to him that the root cause of the problem might have been that he simply didn't believe that what he was teaching these students was the most important thing they were going to learn that day. To his credit, he admitted that there was a lot of truth in my comment, saying that, when planning the lesson, he had anticipated that the students would not be interested in what he had to say. He agreed with me that this belief had become a self-fulfilling prophesy. He had taught with little conviction and enthusiasm, and the students had responded accordingly. My response was to tell him that teachers need to be like actors. Actors don't always feel like 'turning it on', but it is important for them to remember that they have a duty to the audience to perform. The same responsibility applies to the student 'audience' in a class. We all have bad days when we really don't feel particularly inspirational, or when we are teaching potentially 'boring' topics. Students will forgive this now and again, especially in lessons where we have built up good working relationships with them. However, if you are a beginning teacher, you might experience problems with your classes unless you bear this issue in mind. The sign of a good teacher is someone who is able to enthuse students about the most mundane topics, and convince them that what they are learning is the most important thing since 'sliced bread'.

What absolutely shouts out from these findings is the importance of encouragement and of a teacher's belief in the individual student. Never underestimate the positive effect of a hand on the shoulder and an encouraging word of praise. As obvious as this advice sounds, I still feel it needs to be said. I received so many descriptions of teachers who failed to do this and, as a result, failed to inspire and motivate their students.

Organization, efficiency, classroom control and good pedagogy

Another major criterion of a good teacher that emanated from these responses relates to the issues of classroom management and good pedagogy.

> Very strict, but fair. Insisted that everyone did their best.
> My geography teacher had excellent class control – she planned the lessons well and made the lessons relevant.

The class I was in for biology had it in several boys whose behaviour was not particularly good (our year being the first one to stay on after the fourth year – a gloomy prospect for the local lads who just wanted to leave in January/February and go out to work). With her experience in dealing with 'streetwise' city children, Miss X's powers of discipline were superb. She handled these difficult characters with humour and firm approach and her teaching was inspirational to say the least.

My English teacher's lessons were perfect. When she entered the room she only had to sit on the desk at the front of the room and the class felt silent – out of respect and anticipation, not out of fear of reprisal.

My history teacher was quite a scary and formidable man with such a quiet voice – you had to be quiet to hear what he said.

My geography teacher was always fair, always in control – we always knew what the 'deal' was.

My favourite teachers were firm and assertive – you knew where you were with them and that you would be able to get on in their lessons.

My Latin and General Studies teacher had an open mind, always made you think, had great debates, never had preconceived ideas but always challenged you to support your views.

I have long been of the opinion that even the most disruptive students actually want their teachers to take control in the classroom and to challenge them academically. My long-standing experience and recent research show me that these students respect the teachers who manage to do this successfully. Much of this control is down to a teacher's assertive use of body language, eye contact and tone of voice, all of which are discussed later in this book. Much was said in the questionnaire responses about remembering teachers simply because they were 'fun'. The following quotes are a selective sample of these responses:

Using creativity and a sense of humour to make lessons fun

My chemistry teacher, Mr X was always firm but fair . . . he would also talk about other things with us. e.g. We had a Polo sucking competition in A Level Chemistry.

I remember Mr X because he was the stereotypical 'mad scientist' type! Very funny and very eccentric. He even looked like 'Mr Tefal Man'.

I remember Mrs X, my Biology teacher – she was nice, funny and a good laugh. She was a good teacher.

Mr X was very funny, loved his subject, brought it alive and was a bit of an actor. Involved me in a funny production of a play in Spanish in the Sixth Form. Also told us funny anecdotes about his family life.

My favourite teacher at secondary school was Mrs X who taught me English. What I mostly remember was her sarcastic and sharp sense of humour which was quick and intelligent.

I remember Mr X for his terrible jokes – he could be strict but you knew where you stood. He encouraged everyone in the class to take part and made it clear that your contributions were valuable. When work was done well you really felt that it was appreciated. The main thing was he made me feel that I could be successful if I was prepared to put the work in. He proved a turning point in my school career and now in my working life – thank you! I can't remember a thing he taught me though – but I do remember the jokes – it's almost as if I still hear them!

I remember Mr X who taught me in the last year of primary school. He told us fantastic stories about his life and all the amazing experiences he had. I don't think that half of them were true, but they made good stories. We could tell that he loved us and that he enjoyed teaching us.

It is not surprising that so many respondents remembered these teachers for their idiosyncratic ways or sense of fun. You may be aware that there is a part of the brain called the 'limbic system'. Among other functions, this part of the brain deals with emotions and long-term memory. Using humour in the classroom produces a feel-good factor that is retained within the memory for a very long time. That is why it is often easier to remember a teacher being funny or entertaining, rather than to recall what they taught. That is not to say that this knowledge hasn't been retained. It is just that it is harder to locate in memory the specific incidences when it was acquired. As Professor H. Arsham of Baltimore University states:

'Students appreciate a teacher who gives them something to take home to think about besides homework. One often forgets what one was taught. However, one only can make use of what one has learnt.'

(From *Educator as a Midwife*)

What also made teachers memorable to many respondents was their ability to use the personal touch with their students. A small kindness, such as having a cup of coffee and an informal chat with a student, remained in the long-term memory of one respondent in the study.

Another respondent mentions that, when she was a General Certificate of Secondary Education (GCSE) student, she was sick over a piece of art work she needed to turn in, and how her teacher made her a cup of coffee, gave her some time to compose herself, and then extended her deadline by half a day.

Still another respondent recalls that she received a postcard from her language teacher wishing her luck just before her external exams. She went on to say that she has adopted this practice with her own students.

Although I want to offer positive role models to you as beginning teachers, I was not able to ignore some of the many responses about bad teachers that emanated from this research. Perhaps one of the most telling comments came from a highly respected and skilled teacher, and Head of Year (HOY), who made the following observation:

> When I was at school I was so appalled by the attitudes of my teachers that I vowed if I ever did end up as a teacher, I would not be like them.

Some stories were even more negative and bizarre than this. For example, the following story comes from the Head of Department (HOD) for English about one of her former English teachers:

> I felt very sorry for Mr X who was one of the real eccentrics of teaching. Close to retirement, he often fell asleep in lessons. I remember one lesson vividly when he instructed us to read Chapter Ten of 'Great Expectations', sat down, fell asleep then woke up before the bell and told us to pack away. We'd kept as quiet as mice so as not to wake him up! He did a lesson on gerunds which I thought was a load of rubbish at the time. Now I know what gerunds are (after 12 years of teaching A Level students) but I still think the lesson was irrelevant!
>
> I also remember the names of the rotten teachers and their poor attitudes, lack of fairness, bullying and the distaste they had for students – very sad people.
>
> Real cow – told me I would never amount to anything! She slapped me over my hands. I proved her wrong!

My form teacher in Year 10 enjoyed inflicting punishment and took pleasure from his form watching the punishment being inflicted. I tend to recall those who failed rather than those who succeeded. Mr X (Physics) said there was nobody capable of passing O' Level and refused to teach it. After much pressure, he agreed to let me take the exam but refused to teach me – he just gave me the books and told me to get on with it.

The message that really comes through from this research is that children have amazingly long memories. We need to think very carefully about our body language, our tone of voice and about how we speak to our young people. I often tell my beginning teachers that if they treat their Year Seven students with kindness, respect, fairness and firmness, they are likely to have very few behavioural issues with these youngsters as they move up through the school. The following Chinese proverb puts these sentiments in a slightly more erudite fashion but the message is still the same: 'A youth is to be regarded with respect. How do you know that his future will not be equal to our present?' (Confucius). We don't always get things right! We are only human after all. However, if we do get things wrong then we need to hold our hands up to our mistakes and make the situation good with our students. If we fail to do this, then their negative memories of us as teachers will stay with them for a long time.

Suggestions

- Use your memories of good teachers to inform your practice
- Think back to the bad teachers who taught you – learn from their mistakes
- Teach with honesty and passion
- Hold high expectations of your students and of yourself
- Marry teacher warmth, humour and care with a firm hand
- Nurture and develop the actor in you

How do you want to be remembered?

2

What kind of teacher are you?

You may recall from reading the introduction that I described the one piece of academic research I hold particularly dear – the work of Zimpher and Howey. In their 1987 paper, they write at length about what they call the 'personal domain' of a teacher. It is this domain that forms the specific focus of this chapter. Here, the conception of a teacher is one of a 'self-actualized person' who uses himself/herself as an effective and humane instrument of classroom instruction. The term 'self-actualized' strongly implies that a teacher possesses a high level of self-knowledge. You might be forgiven for asking how the acquisition of self-knowledge can help teachers to establish, maintain and develop good relationships with their students. My response is simple. Competence in this domain requires teachers to fully develop and hone their intra-personal skills. They can do this by raising their level of self-awareness, and by being critical in their analysis of their relationships with other people. Full competence in this domain, therefore, requires teachers to fully understand the interactional nature of teaching. Knowledge of one's strengths, weaknesses and emotional needs can allow teachers to make informed decisions about the ways in which they deal with their students. This then allows them to provide a warm and supportive learning environment. The aim of this chapter is, therefore, to facilitate a scenario whereby you, as a beginning teacher, can ask yourself questions and explore the impact of your teaching style on your relationships with your students.

One of the first issues to focus on is that of self-esteem. Simply put, teachers with high self-esteem produce students with high self-esteem. Unfortunately, however, the converse is also true. It is fair to say that people with low self-esteem do not value their personal qualities, nor do they see themselves as being very capable. Often this view is contrary to the way others see them.

I have found that teachers with low self-esteem tend to be defensive, extremely sensitive to criticizm, and rather intolerant of alternative view-points. Very often they see an attempt to get them to practise reflectivity, as a personal slight on their teaching capabilities. So, how do these behaviours impact their relationships with students? Put quite simply, these teachers struggle to establish and maintain meaningful learning relationships with their students. What these teachers tend to do is to *personalize* students' inappropriate behaviour, and to view this as a personal attack on them, rather than as a manifestation of any inner difficulties the student concerned may be experiencing. A teacher with low self-esteem often finds it very difficult to distance himself from the student's poor behaviour. In other words, they see everything that happens in the classroom as being about themselves, and not about the students. A particular example that comes to mind is where a young teacher overheard one of his students saying that he 'hated' him. This NQT, who had only been teaching for about a term, understandably became quite upset about this remark, reacted angrily, and took the incident as a personal affront to his professionalism. My role was to try to get the NQT to take a step back from the incident, and to get him to view this inappropriate behaviour from the student's perspective. I tried to get him to see that there is usually a rationale and a history behind the inappropriate actions of stu-dents. I told this teacher that, if the student had a negative feeling towards him, then it was important to find out why this was the case, and to then try to tackle the issues that were bothering this youngster. I asked the NQT to adopt an 'inquisitorial' rather than 'adversarial' stance and to discuss the issue with the student. I asked him to think carefully about the body language he used when talking to this youngster, and to remember that a discussion involves listening as well as speaking. The NQT did this and soon came back to me in a very different frame of mind. It turned out that the youngster had been annoyed and hurt because he felt he had been humiliated in front of the class for not doing his homework properly, and for being made to do the work again. Both the teacher and the boy learned something from this incident. The teacher learned that using sarcasm and ridicule to belittle a student in class, in order 'to score points' with the other students, was unacceptable and coun-terproductive. He also began to understand that this incident had occurred primarily because of his high level of uncertainty and low self-esteem in this particular situation. He was fairly new to this class and was worried about the lack of homework coming in from students. He had taken this as a per-sonal slight. As their discussion unfurled, the student began to see things from the teacher's perspective, and learned some alternative ways of dealing with issues such as these. I can assure you that these types of situations don't just happen to inexperienced teachers. In one of my classes, for example, I suddenly began to feel a degree of antipathy towards me from one of my Year Ten students, with whom, up to this point, I had got on quite well. Let's call her Kate. There was nothing overtly aggressive about her behaviour, but I just had a 'gut feeling' that things were not quite right. Having looked at her prior attainment data, I knew that she was seriously underachieving, so I decided to talk to her about it one evening after school. Kate was initially quite defensive and didn't really want to talk about the issue. At this point I had to reassure her that however personal her remarks might be, and whatever she had to say, I would try not to take offence. I added that I just needed to know what was going on. By using a non-confrontational tone of voice and sympathetic body language, I found out the root cause of the issue. It turned out that her sister and my daughter had fallen out, and she felt that because of this I didn't like her. I was absolutely amazed at this disclosure, but fortunately, I managed to dispel these preconceptions, and things soon returned to normal. I need to make two points about this incident; had I not had the confidence to try to ascertain the history and rationale behind Kate's behaviour, perhaps these bad feelings would have festered and our relationship would have broken down completely. In my early years of teaching, I would not have been secure enough, nor would I have had the self-esteem to open up such a can of worms. Over the course of my teaching career I have trained myself to deal with situations such as these with, hopefully, a reasonable degree of success.

Having tutored dozens of beginning teachers, I realize that the development of self-esteem is not necessarily an exponential process. If self-esteem could be charted on a graph, it would not appear as a smooth continuum. It is more likely that the graph would show a series of peaks and troughs showing periods of real self-belief and confidence, and periods of great self-doubt and depression. Hopefully, however, one would expect an overall rise in teacher confidence and self-esteem, correlating with increasing levels of experience. It is not within the remit of this book to explore the general psychological reasons behind a teacher's lack of esteem, so I have, therefore, limited my discussion to those factors affected by the teacher's experience in schools. The acquisition of high self-esteem depends on a number of things: the personality of the teacher, the experiences of the teacher within their school, and the level of formal and informal support the teacher receives from their colleagues. It would also be highly hypocritical of me to say that well-established and successful members of the teaching staff do not experience self-doubt and periods of low self-esteem. Of course they do, but the more secure teachers learn from their experiences and manage to get to grips with these feelings sooner rather than later, and then simply manage to get on with the job. Very often, it is through dealing with specific incidents reflectively that we learn how to increase our self-esteem. So, what advice would I offer beginning teachers on how to deal with potentially difficult incidents, while at the same time developing and maintaining one's self-esteem?

- Be aware that you could be personalizing issues, and try to step back from the incident and view the situation with the needs of the student in mind.
- Try not to react to external pressures while dealing with the student or with specific incidents. For example, try not to worry too much about how some of your more robust colleagues may view the way you deal with difficult situations.
- Try to get behind the words and the body language of the student you are dealing with. Ascertain what these verbal and non-verbal signals are saying about the person sending the message. Find out their needs from the conversation.
- Once you have found out the needs of the student, try to respond to them appropriately. It may be something you can deal with immediately, or it may require a degree of planning, or, alternatively, you may need to seek the assistance of more experienced professional. Accepting that you cannot deal with some issues on your own is an important learning point.
- Ensure the student knows that you will always be there for him /her. Do not close all lines of communication. Remember that some students prefer to write things down, so you may need to give them the opportunity to do this. However, be very careful about the issue of 'disclosure'. Inform the youngster that you may have to pass on sensitive information to the Head of Year.
- Make sure you hold on to your self-esteem. The specific issue should be about the student, not you.
- Above all, make sure you learn from the experience. If you follow the advice offered here, you will be.able to deal with the incident more successfully than if you simply go in with 'all guns blazing'. Take heart from this; congratulate yourself; make a conscious effort to elevate your self-esteem; be accepting of yourself when things don't quite go according to plan; mentally reflect on what you could have done differently; accept that mistakes are opportunities for learning. By doing this you will remain in control of the process – it is this control that will help to reinforce your self-esteem.

Humphries (1996 and 1998) describes how teachers with low- to middle-level self-esteem tend to 'project' when dealing with students in their charge. What he means by this is that the teacher puts the responsibility for their own lives onto their students. For example, if I say, 'you're really getting me down', I am giving you a lot of power over me, and relinquishing my own responsibility for my own needs. Let's be honest here, we have all had classes where individual students have really 'got to us'; where they have evoked strong feelings of impotence; where they have done their best to undermine our authority; where they seem to be able to set the agenda for the lesson. In other words, when these youngsters are absent from the class, we are different and more confident teachers. It is difficult for any teacher to deal with students like this, let alone a beginning teacher. Much of the issue lies with the self-esteem of the teacher. Although he or she is probably unable to articulate this, the student has managed to find the vulnerabilities and the low self-esteem of the teacher, and has then 'gone in for the kill'. This type of student can evoke two extreme reactions from teachers with low self-esteem. They are either allowed to have the run of the classroom, doing just what they want, or they enter into a power struggle with the teacher. Neither scenario is beneficial to the teacher nor to the student. Often, merely understanding the issue can help a teacher to adopt a more balanced perspective of the problem, and allow them to deal with the student in a more objective and distanced manner. By employing this approach, the inappropriate behaviour is focused on, and not the student's character traits. I have often found that 'stepping back' in dealing with individual students such as these, using the methods prescribed here, reduces the tension, and harmony is, once again, restored.

So how does all of this marry with the main theme of the book – that of establishing, maintaining and developing relationships with students? Quite simply, the more skilled a teacher becomes in raising their self-esteem, the more they will be able to deal positively with their students. It is a mistake, therefore, to think that the only people who need developing are the students. Teaching is an interactive process – both parties need to learn and to grow.

To help beginning teachers to do just this, I have provided a set of descriptions of teacher–student relationships that are based on the excellent work of Tony Humphries (1996 and 1998), who has identified six types of teacher–student relationships. Descriptions of each type can be seen in Figure 2.1. Alongside each description I have included a list of questions for you to think about.

L O W T E A C H E R S E L F- E S T E E M	CHARACTERISTICS	QUESTIONS TO ASK YOURSELF
	Absence of relationship In this classroom the teacher tends to teach the class as a whole and fails to make any real meaningful relationships with any of the students. The question that must arise here is what are they doing in teaching?	**Is this you?** Do you recognize any of these characteristics in your teaching? Are there any students in your classes who you do not have a good working relationship with? What have you done about it? Do you recognize these characteristics in other teachers you know? How do you feel about these teachers?
	Relationship devoid of feeling It is recognized that this teacher is a good technician in as much as they prepare their lessons well and provide the necessary material required for academic success. They are good disciplinarians and experience very few problems in the classroom. However, the teacher shows little obvious warmth and/or closeness to students. The teacher is simply there to teach.	**Is this you?** Do you recognize any of these characteristics in your teaching? Do you focus too much on the technical side of teaching? (Technical Domain) Do you need to develop the Personal Domain? Do you need to give more attention to how you teach rather than what you teach? Do you understand the full role of the teacher? How are aware are you of the different types of intelligences? Do you cater for these in your lesson planning? What satisfaction do you get out of teaching? Do you recognize these characteristics in other teachers you know? What do you think of these teachers?
	Narcissistic relationship This type of teacher does establish relationships with their students but these are very much conditional. When the student meets the teacher's needs, they gain approval. Failure to meet their demands will lead to a breakdown of relationships and negativity from the teacher. In this relationship the standard of students' behaviour becomes the key method of measuring their worth.	**Is this you?** Are your relationships with students conditional? Do you recognize any of these characteristics in your teaching? Do you enjoy good working relationships with students who don't think like you? Do you have pro-school and anti-school sub-cultures within your classes? What do you do about this? Does your lesson planning cater for the interests of all students in your classes? Do you recognize these characteristics in other teachers you know? What do you think of these teachers?

Figure 2.1 Professional esteem levels and teaching styles

	Over-involved relationships	Is this you?
	This type of teacher really 'needs to be needed' and will go to extremes in order to be needed by their students. This teacher feels they are indispensable and will work extra long hours and/or take on far more than they should in order to develop this indispensability. Very often this is all done at a sub-conscious level but the strong message to their students is that, as long as you value me for what I do for you, I will accept and approve of you. Students who reject these conditions and/or students, who prefer to be independent decision-makers, are likely to be rejected by this teacher.	Do you recognize any of these characteristics in your teaching? Do you try to interfere in the personal lives of your students? Do you hold on to information that really needs to be shared? Do you take on responsibility at school in order to be needed? Do you take time off work when you need to? Are you able to delegate? Do you overtly seek approval from your students? Do you fish for compliments from your students? Do you enjoy good relationships with students who don't appear to need you? Do you enjoy good relationships with students who don't think like you? Do you recognize these characteristics in other teachers you know? What do you think of these teachers?
	Symbiotic relationships	Is this you?
	In this teacher's class there is very little room for individuality. The teacher holds a corporate view of the class whereby the students' needs are subjugated in order to serve the 'whole'. Interdependence rather than independence is highly valued. In this situation, each student requires the approval of both teacher and other students to feel valued. As a result of this, student self-esteem is low.	Do you recognize any of these characteristics in your teaching? Do you use the corporate power of the class to impose disapproval on sanction breakers? Do you show respect and approval for those students who 'break the mould'? Do you enjoy good working relationships with students who don't think like you? Do you recognize these characteristics in other teachers you know? What do you think of these teachers?
HIGH TEACHER	Empathic relationship	Is this you?
	The teacher enjoys a healthy relationship with his students. Relationships are of an unconditional nature where each student is valued for themselves irrespective of their social background, academic ability and attitude towards school. This teacher shows an interest in students because they value and respect them for their uniqueness as human beings.	Do you recognize any of these characteristics in your teaching? Do you value all the students in your classes or do you let some 'slip through the net'? How important is the delivery of subject knowledge in your lessons? Is the student/teacher relationship the most important facet of your teaching? How do you show your students that you understand their uniqueness as individuals? Do you impose your sanctions within a warm caring and affirming framework?

Figure 2.1 *Contd.*

| S E L F- E S T E E M | This type of teacher is known as an 'affirming teacher' because he values the relationship with the student above all else. No amount of inappropriate behaviour, mistakes or failures will break that relationship. This teacher, however, is not a 'soft touch'. They hold strong views about what constitutes acceptable and non-acceptable behaviour but any sanctions imposed are carried out within a framework of a warm affirming relationship. The teacher takes every opportunity to help the student learn to take responsibility for his, or her, own actions. The teacher does not overtly criticize or put down students nor do they use sarcasm to try to change their behaviour. This teacher shows they value the student by giving them a chance to make a constructive contribution to any sanctions imposed. | Do you give your students an opportunity to make a constructive contribution to disciplinary procedures? Do you recognize these characteristics in other teachers you know? What do you think of these teachers? |

Figure 2.1 *Contd*

As helpful as the descriptions shown in Figure 2.1 be, it also needs to be said that placing teacher behaviour into categories can be somewhat problematic. I challenge any teacher, experienced or otherwise, to say that their teaching behaviour fits neatly into any single category. In my opinion, we can all identify elements of our teaching in each one of the categories described above at some point in our teaching careers. I would even go so far as to say that, during a typical academic year, even the most talented and gifted teachers fail to realize the empathic-relationship criteria more than 80 per cent of the time. We are all human; we all have 'off-days', and we cannot be expected to reach this high standard day after day. What is important, however, is for us to be fully aware of the impact that our behaviours can have on our students, and for us to try hard not to behave towards them in inappropriate and potentially damaging ways. However, this should not be seen as a one-way process! Your students too have a large part to play here. They have to realize that people in the adult world, as represented in school by teachers, are different from each other. An invaluable part of the hidden curriculum is the students' gradual realization that they have to make many adjustments to the varying demands of teachers in school. It is part of their preparation for adult life and, as such, is as important as maths, English and science. They learn that there are some teachers they like and others they cannot stand the sight of; that some teachers appear to like them and that others do not.

Styles of management and teaching

One of things you as beginning teachers have to decide is the management and teaching style you are going to employ in the classroom. Your choice of style determines the climate of your classroom and, ultimately, the quality of your relationships with your students. I have used, and adapted, the work of K. Lewin (1939), cited in Rogers (2011), to draw up a continuum of possible teaching styles. This is shown in Figure 2.2. Read through the text and try to ascertain where you currently fit along this continuum.

Lewin uses the term 'laissez- faire' to describe a teaching style that is not supported by rules and routines, firm expectations and sanctions, and where pretty much 'anything goes'. As useful as this contribution is, I am not totally happy with this description because I feel that there are many teachers who do have good intentions, who do outline their expectations and who do employ sanctions, but who fail to do so consistently. In my opinion, it is this inconsistency and indecisiveness that undermines good teacher–student relationships. Students simply do not know where they stand. For the purposes of this book, therefore, I refer to this type as 'indecisive' teachers. I have put together a composite portrait of a typical lesson taught by an indecisive teacher.

The indecisive teacher

Teacher X is a nice man who wants to be liked and who really wants to succeed as a maths teacher. He has planned the content of his lesson reasonably well, but knows from the start that things are not going to go according to plan. He is expecting trouble from a group of boys in his Year Nine class but, although, he has received plenty of advice from colleagues, he has not

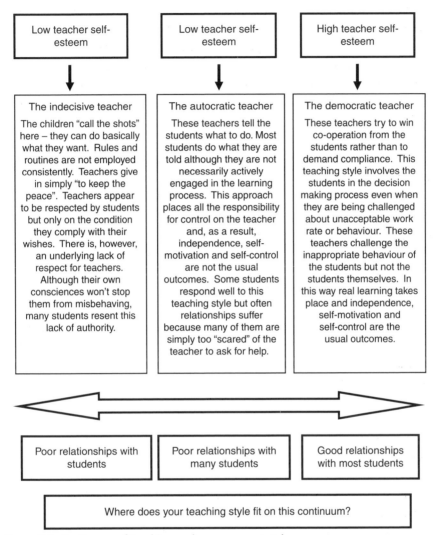

Continuum of Teaching and Management Styles

Low teacher self-esteem	Low teacher self-esteem	High teacher self-esteem
The indecisive teacher The children "call the shots" here – they can do basically what they want. Rules and routines are not employed consistently. Teachers give in simply "to keep the peace". Teachers appear to be respected by students but only on the condition they comply with their wishes. There is, however, an underlying lack of respect for teachers. Although their own consciences won't stop them from misbehaving, many students resent this lack of authority.	**The autocratic teacher** These teachers tell the students what to do. Most students do what they are told although they are not necessarily actively engaged in the learning process. This approach places all the responsibility for control on the teacher and, as a result, independence, self-motivation and self-control are not the usual outcomes. Some students respond well to this teaching style but often relationships suffer because many of them are simply too "scared" of the teacher to ask for help.	**The democratic teacher** These teachers try to win co-operation from the students rather than to demand compliance. This teaching style involves the students in the decision making process even when they are being challenged about unacceptable work rate or behaviour. These teachers challenge the inappropriate behaviour of the students but not the students themselves. In this way real learning takes place and independence, self-motivation and self-control are the usual outcomes.

Poor relationships with students	Poor relationships with many students	Good relationships with most students

Where does your teaching style fit on this continuum?

Figure 2.2 Continuum of teaching and management styles

arrived at the lesson with any definite strategies for dealing with potential disruption.

Class 9Y enter the room very noisily. That's OK, they will settle down soon, thinks Mr X who puts his head down and busies himself by flicking through some papers on his desk. The students don't settle down. Mr X is getting a little worried about the noise level in the room. It is an old classroom, with high ceilings, and he is concerned that his colleagues in the adjacent rooms will hear the noise. What will they think of him? 'Sshssh', he says in a pleading voice, 'will you please keep quiet now? Please settle down'. The noise continues. In desperation, he pleads, 'If you keep making that noise you won't be able to play the game I've got planned for you'. Eventually, after a great deal of effort, Mr X recognizes a lull in the noise level and feels he is ready to move on. 'Quiet, please, while I take the register', says Mr X who has his pen in his hand and who has his head down, looking at his mark book. Most of the students eventually comply with his request, but, yes, you guessed it, the Mafia in the back row are having none of it, and carry on talking. Mr X takes the register even though many of the students are still chatting to each other and are generally 'larking about'.

'Right, this is what we are going to do today' says Mr X cheerfully. 'First, I am going to check that you understood the equations we did yesterday, and then we are going to do some more book work. If you are good, then we will play a mathematical game for the last fifteen minutes of the lesson'.

Instead of Mr X *asking* the students how to do the equations, he *tells* them how they are done while writing some examples on the board. As soon as he turns away from the class, the boys on the back row start talking loudly and hitting each other. 'Quiet boys, please', shouts Mr X, getting more and more exasperated. 'It's not fair on the others – if you don't behave yourself, the class won't get their game'. 'It's not our fault', one of the boys, Gary, says. 'We don't understand the work. You never help us!' he shouts. 'Why do you have to be so rude Gary? Would you talk to your mother like that'? 'Yes, I would' Gary yells out laughingly, looking around for an audience to share the joke with. 'Well, the reason you don't understand this work is simply because you weren't listening when I was explaining things to you', said Mr X. 'You were messing about at the back'. 'No, we weren't, we couldn't hear you – you were turning away from us. It's not our fault. You always pick on us. You can ask anyone. Ask Dawn – she'll tell you'! 'He's right sir, you do pick on them' piped up Dawn. 'Leave him alone, he's only trying to do his job' yells out Teresa, who is getting fed up with the whole business. 'Just be quiet both of you and let me explain the work' shouts Mr X, who is getting increasingly hot under the collar. 'Bloody hell, I'm only trying to help you', shouts Teresa aggressively. 'I won't bother in future'. 'Please don't use language like that Teresa. You should know better. Your mum didn't bring you up like that'. 'You don't know anything about my family'! snarls Teresa. Fifteen minutes has passed, the lesson has degenerated into chaos, and no learning has yet taken place. The same pattern continues for the rest of the lesson – but, in order to keep the peace, Mr X allows the students to have their game, which lasts half an hour, not the fifteen minutes he promised at the beginning of the lesson. In order to make amends for the way the lesson has gone, he makes Dawn, Gary and Teresa team captains for the game.

Mr X left the classroom exhausted and demoralized. He had failed because he was unable to realize his lesson objectives and because he had got angry with the class. Needless to say, the group of boys at the back enjoyed the lesson immensely.

The question we have to ask ourselves is why Mr X's indecisive teaching style was so ineffective. I have outlined the reasons as follows:

- He did not come to the lesson with any behaviour-management strategies in mind. He knew there were going to be problems, but felt it was beyond his capabilities to prevent them.
- His tone of voice and body language were not assertive enough and showed indecision and prevarication on his part.
- He did not dominate the teaching space sufficiently enough to be listened to by his students.
- He became entwined in the students' secondary behaviour – the arguments with Gary, Dawn and Teresa got out of hand simply because he didn't cut the discussion short.
- He simply failed to impose his will on the students.
- He showed his displeasure too late and, as a result, was left with few options but to shout at the class.
- Despite all his good intentions, he allowed the students to set the agenda for the lesson. Not only did they get their game even though they had behaved inappropriately, but Mr X extended the time allocation for it by fifteen minutes, simply to keep the peace and to calm things down. He rewarded the bad behaviour of the three miscreants by appointing them as team captains.
- He hoped for compliance, believing that his friendliness and reasonableness would win the students round. This simply didn't happen. He also hoped that his goodwill gesture of extending the game would make the students like him and that, because of this, they would do the work. This didn't happen either.

Do you recognize any of your teaching behaviours in Figure 2.2?

The autocratic teacher

There are certain teachers in most schools whom students simply don't mess with. If these teachers have a bad day, then everybody knows it!

Mr Y enters the room. By the time he has walked to the front of the class-room, most of the students are quiet and ready to listen attentively. However, there are a couple of students 'chancing their arms' at the back of the room by finishing off their conversation. Mr Y could have ignored this but chose not to. 'Hey, you two'! shouts Mr Y who stares fiercely at the two youngsters. 'How dare you talk when I come into the room! You two are always talking when you shouldn't be. How many times do I have to tell you about this! Don't do that again! Understand'! 'Yes' the two students say rather sulkily. 'Yes sir!' shouts Mr Y. 'Yes sir,' they comply.

Mr Y starts the lesson but is interrupted by the two at the back smiling at each other. This is not a good move. It's time for a showdown. 'Who do you two think you are'? he yells. He thinks, this is my lesson and no one does that to me. 'Do that again and I'll come down on you like a ton of bricks'! The rest of the students start to fidget uncomfortably and look nervously at Mr Y. He moves the students away from each other to different parts of the room.

Mr Y explains the work once, and then circulates around the classroom checking that students are on task. When he gets to each of the two miscre-ants, he stands behind them in an attempt to intimidate them and to show them who is the boss. When he has made his point, he returns to the front of the room, where he sits down for most of the remainder of the lesson. If he hears someone talking, even quietly, he makes a sarcastic and caustic com-ment designed to embarrass the students concerned.

Mr Y is also not averse to using insults to put his students down. 'Are you thick, boy'? He yells at a student who tells him he doesn't understand the work and who has been asking his neighbour for advice. As he looks up, he notices that Michael has got black trainers on. 'What are those things you've got on your feet'? he yells at Michael fiercely. 'They're trainers sir, but they're black, just like shoes. I've got my old shoes in my locker but they're falling apart. My mum says she'll get some shoes for Monday when she gets her benefits, but that I'm to wear these for the time being'. 'Go and change those now, Michael'. 'But sir, I can't wear my old shoes, they're falling apart'. 'I don't care, go and change them or else you'll have me to answer to'. 'I'm not changing them sir. I have explained why I can't put my shoes on. They're falling apart! I've told you, sir'! Mr Y begins to realize that someone has to back down here and it's not going to be him. 'Go to your Head of Year', he yells slamming a textbook down on the desk. 'If you are in my classroom, you obey my rules! If you don't like my rules, you can stand outside the classroom for the rest of the lesson. It makes no difference to me!'

On the face of it, Mr Y appears to be an effective teacher. He doesn't get much trouble from students – his reputation sees to that. Mr Y is proud of his standing within the school. If you pass his room, the students all appear to be working and, above all, to be behaving themselves. It would also be quite understandable for a beginning teacher, who, believing that a quiet classroom is a learning classroom, would aspire to establishing a similar disciplinary hold over their students. The question you need to ask, however, is whether this is an effective classroom environment for real learning to take place. The teacher–student relationship in this classroom is one of fear, not respect. Mr Y doesn't respect his students and the students most certainly do not respect Mr Y. The dominant climate in this classroom is adversarial, with Mr Y feeling that the students should obey him at all times and that he should win every discipline battle he encounters during the course of his normal teaching day. Mr Y is a teacher with low self-esteem who is frightened to let things go, even a little. He is worried that if he relinquishes his control over the students, then chaos will reign and he will be left alone with his vulnerabilities.

There is nothing wrong in a teacher being demanding. Nor is there any issue about a teacher being authoritative when they need to be. That is all part of the job. However, an authoritarian and autocratic teacher like Mr Y does the profession a great disservice. His overbearing, sarcastic and aggressive attitude has the effect of stripping his students of their self-esteem, dignity and rights as human beings. There is no way that real learning can take place in this kind of setting. Autocratic teachers like Mr Y:

- don't like children
- demand compliance from their students
- see the classroom as a war zone, with them as the eventual victors
- give orders to students, rather than asking them to do things
- don't allow students to make choices
- verbally threaten the students on a regular basis
- nag and preach to students
- use sarcasm, humiliation and verbal aggression as a means of class control
- rarely smile or share a joke

- laugh *at* students but not *with* them
- make inappropriate personal remarks about the students
- engender fear, not respect.

Do you recognize any of your teaching behaviours here?

I suspect that, in the past, autocratic teachers like Mr Y would probably have resorted to physical sanctions to discipline students. This might have been done formally, through the use of the school's corporal punishment system, or, more likely, by some form of physical assault on the students. As tempting as it may be at times, you are strongly advised to keep your hands off your students. In a world of increasing litigation, you would do well to be extremely circumspect about the use of physical force and to heed the advice offered in this extract from the guidelines of the National Union of Teachers (NUT).

ADVICE ON THE PHYSICAL RESTRAINT OF STUDENTS

The NUT advises that teachers should not intervene without help unless in their professional judgement such intervention is unavoidable. Teachers should not intervene unless they feel confident and comfortable in so doing. Where the risk is not urgent, teachers should consider carefully whether and when physical intervention is appropriate. Teachers should make every reasonable effort to summon assistance as soon as possible. The NUT advises that teachers should not intervene in situations where they feel such action might place them at risk professionally or physically. The NUT advises that members should not use physical restraint unless they have undergone training and are aware of the school policy.

In circumstances where teachers believe they or other students may be at risk of injury, the teacher should remove those students who might be at risk and summon assistance from colleagues. Where necessary, through the senior leadership team, the police should be contacted. The complexity and range of need and consequent support for children and young people with severe and/or complex learning difficulties, including autism, may be such that physical intervention is the norm and not the exception. Thus low and medium level intervention would not always be recorded. This would most likely be recorded and monitored through the young person's IEP. Staff who teach students

---

with Autistic Spectrum Disorders or learning disabilities should refer to the joint DCSF and Department of Health guidance for physical intervention for students with Autistic Spectrum Disorders.

Source: **From the National Union of Teachers webpage** (www. teachers.org.uk/files/Student-Behaviour-5427.pdf

Guidance on what to do when such risks become apparent is set out under the link on student exclusions which can also be found on this website.

The democratic teacher

The democratic teacher is the successful teacher. You should aspire to this teaching style if you want to develop good learning relationships with your students. Although many teachers develop the democratic style as they become more experienced, you don't necessarily have to be 'old' to be a decisive, democratic teacher. I come across many teachers who display many of those qualities required to be a democratic teacher, either in their induction year or certainly after a few years of teaching. Conversely, I have also encountered a lot of older, so-called more experienced teachers, whose teaching style is far from democratic, and who are unlikely ever to be able to adopt this approach with their students. It is, therefore, all about having the right attitude and showing a willingness to reflect positively on your teaching, and on your interactions with your students. Miss Z is one such teacher. She is a young geography teacher who has been teaching in the same school for the past four years. She would, however, be the first to admit that earlier on in her career, she made a number of basic mistakes. When looking back over her brief teaching career, she realized that she simply hadn't been authoritative enough with her students during her first two years at the school. She would also accept that, in those early days, much of her teaching behaviour matched the description of the typically indecisive teacher given to you earlier in this chapter. Things are very different now. What happened for her to be able to turn things around so dramatically? Despite being told repeatedly about the importance of establishing rules and routines in her classroom, and of being objective and consistent when dealing with disciplinary issues, she only really took this on board towards the end of her second year. Her way simply wasn't working and she began to realize that things had to change. It seems that it took almost two years for Miss Z to internalize all the advice and guidance given to her, and to fully understand the rationale behind the school's induction programme. She is now already well on the way to becoming an extremely decisive and democratic teacher and a well-respected member of staff. So what exactly, are the characteristics of a democratic teacher? The following description will give you a flavour of the classroom atmosphere engendered by such a teacher.

Miss Z developed clear rules and routines for her Year Nine class at the beginning of the year. Up to now, this has paid dividends as far as student behaviour is concerned. However, she now senses that the 'honeymoon period' is over, and that some of the students are beginning to misbehave and to 'try their luck' in her lessons.

Miss Z stands in the middle of the room, adopts a positive and confident body posture and scans the class, who now are expecting her to speak. 'Right Class 9M, put your equipment down and look this way. I said look this way! I want to make eye contact with every single one of you.' After about thirty seconds, and a lot of scanning by Miss Z, the students all comply with her instructions.

'I have to say that I have been extremely pleased with the way you have all settled into this class. Your work has been of a good standard and, generally speaking, you have all shown a pretty good attitude towards learning, and towards the rules and routines we agreed on at the beginning of the year. You may remember that we discussed the reasons why we have these rules – to allow everybody to reach their potential in a comfortable and pleasant learning environment. However, I have become a little concerned recently that some of you are going off the boil, in terms of your behaviour and attitudes towards your work. I feel, therefore, that it is now time for us to revisit those rules, routines and expectations. We're going to do this as a quiz and there will be a small prize of a chocolate bar for the top two students. After this, we will get on with the main thrust of the lesson, that is, to explore the effects of locating a superstore near an already congested area of the town. So, will you please get your books out and we can make a start. Thank you.'

Miss Z is happy to use up the twenty minutes or so it will take to reinforce her expectations. She knows that making this investment now will save her a lot of time and effort chasing up on inevitable discipline or work-related problems at a later date. She was so sure about doing this, that she wrote this activity into her lesson plan. The quiz goes well and, having dispensed with the chocolate bars, Miss Z is ready to launch the lesson.

Miss Z simply stands at the front of the class, scanning the students and making calming signals with her hands. The majority of the students become quiet. The remainder fall into line on her verbal cue; 'Right, we are ready to start now – everything down, eyes forward, and give me your full attention please'. This does the trick and very soon all students become attentive. Rather than launching straight into the lesson objectives, Miss Z asks the class the following question: 'Who lives near to a superstore, or who has visited anyone living near to a superstore'? Bearing in mind that there is a superstore within the catchment area, she is on fairly 'safe ground' in using this question to launch the topic. Virtually all the hands go up in response. Miss Z also puts her hand up. (This is a deliberate ploy on her part to create a sense of corporate identity within the class.) At this point, Miss Z thanks the students for their answers and then asks them to focus their attention on the lesson objectives that have already been written on the whiteboard. Having read the objectives out to the class, she then asks the students to copy them down into their books. 'We have now seen that many of us live fairly close to a superstore. Now I want you to tell me what's good, and what's bad about living near a superstore. I want to see if you can come up with at least four good things and four bad things. Remember that it is important for you to remember to put your hands up if you want to make a contribution. Jessica and Graham, will you come up to the board to record the responses?' Again, virtually all the students put their hands up. Miss Z repeats or paraphrases the students' responses, and Jessica and Graham write them down on the board. In their sheer enthusiasm to be heard, a number of students shout out their answers. Miss Z, aware that she needs to stamp this behaviour out, stops the class, scans the room, and pauses dramatically before saying: 'Well done to all those students who want to respond, but I need to remind you about our rule for getting heard in this classroom. You must put your hand up if you want to answer a question. Most of you are doing this, but I would like *all* of you to obey this rule. Thank you.' The situation improves dramatically, but there are still a few students who continue to call out their answers. Miss Z, wanting to continue the flow of the lesson, tactically ignores this for a while, and then frowns at the miscreants and puts her fingers to her lips – this seems to do the trick. These students immediately raise their hands. But things are not going perfectly by any means. Aaron is chewing gum, Roger and Alan are looking out of the window, and Sharon is swinging back on her chair. Miss Z clicks her fingers again to gain their attention. She then points her index finger to one of her eyes to convey her demand that the two boys look at her, and she then follows this up with the 'stare'. To stop Sharon swinging on her chair, all Miss Z does is to make eye contact with her, and gestures to Sharon to come to the front of the class. This leaves only Aaron to deal with. She knows Aaron well – she knows that he loves an audience and would absolutely relish having to make the journey up to the front of the room. So, instead of asking him to come to the front of the class to put his gum in the bin, she adopts a different tactic. She takes the bin over to him, gives him a brief smile and looks at him expectantly until he eventually puts his gum in the bin. She then turns away and carries on with the lesson. Because Miss Z has used all these signals before, all four students are in no doubt as to what is expected of them, and they comply with a minimum of fuss. No one has lost face, discipline has been maintained and, very importantly, the flow of the lesson has not been disrupted.

Why does this approach work? Miss Z has learned over the past three years how to develop an authoritative approach towards her teaching. Rogers (2011) and Dixie (2007), describe how the use of such an approach can produce an effective classroom–management scenario, and help to build meaningful relationships with students. Miss Z does a number of things right: she uses an assertive tone of voice; she chooses her words carefully when giving directives to students, she makes optimum use of eye contact; she adopts a confident and positive body posture. By doing this, she conveys her expectation that her students will accept her authority.

Kyriacou, (2009, p. 103) makes the point superbly when he writes; 'If one behaves as though one has authority, it is surprising how far this attitude exerts a momentum of its own, leading students to behave accordingly . . . ' So, what is the difference between an authoritative and an authoritarian teacher?

Authoritarian teachers do not always read the signals correctly – that is why they often experience conflict with the more strong-willed students in their classes. They see the classroom as an arena in which to do battle where they must win at all costs. They do not understand the need to 'tactically withdraw' at certain times, or with certain students. There is nothing more embarrassing than having to witness a major row between a colleague and an angry student, especially when you feel the youngster has been 'pushed into a corner', and where you hold a degree of sympathy for the his, or her, predicament. Authoritative and democratic teachers know their students. They are able to see immediately when a youngster is having a bad day and, although certainly not sanctioning inappropriate behaviour, they are prepared to wait until a later time to deal with it. A confident teacher with high self-esteem can do this. I remember a lecture by Bill Rogers when he was talking about the use of sanctions – he used the phrase 'certainty, not severity'. This advice has stuck in my mind and is something I have tried to incorporate into my teaching and pass on to the beginning teachers in my school. It is important for you to understand that things do not have to be dealt with there and then. When a student is really wound up and ready to 'have a go', it is often advisable to leave things well alone until the student has calmed down. If you are worried about losing face, try to step back and to remember that the student's inappropriate behaviour is not a personal slight on you. In the heat of the moment, however, this is not an easy thing to do. I remember one incident in my first year of secondary school teaching in an extremely challenging school in west London. I had had a run-in with a boy whose behaviour during my lesson had been totally unacceptable. Let's call him Gary. To be honest, I should have kept Gary behind at break and sorted things out quietly and calmly, but because I felt that his misbehaviour was very much a personal attack on me, I didn't want to talk to him. However, I very soon paid for my mistake. I was just about to launch a geography lesson with my Year Ten class, when Gary burst into the room, knocked over a few chairs and started swearing and insulting me. You can imagine that, as a young and inexperienced teacher, I was quite taken aback. In fact, although I tried to appear outwardly calm, I was inwardly shaking. Gary then stormed out of the room. He was excluded for a period of two weeks. I learned two lessons from this experience. First, that I could have prevented the whole incident by dealing with the earlier incident in a more objective and less personalized manner. My personal pride, however, had stood in my way. My second learning experience occurred three years later, after Gary had left school. He took the trouble to come back to see me to tell me how he was getting on. He apologized to me for his outburst and explained to me that his mum and dad had split up the evening before the incident, and that he was angry and simply 'looking for a fight'. I was the first person he had come across. I have to say that I felt very humbled by his apology. 'There is no need for you to apologize to me, Gary', I told him. 'I am the adult, and I should have read the situation better. Please accept *my* apologies'. We parted on very good terms.

You will remember Mr X, the autocratic teacher. He constantly nagged, bullied and preached to his students. Authoritative teachers, such as Miss Z, do not nag or preach. They know that is the worst thing that they can do! Teenagers simply hate nags! You have only got to look at the rolling eyes and negative body language of a student who is being given a right good scolding by the school nag, to see the effect it can have on the teacher–student relationship, and subsequently on learning. Authoritative teachers generally keep calm, refer to previously launched rules, and, to ensure maximum impact, keep their admonitions to an absolute minimum. They do attack students personally, but prefer instead to make the unacceptability of the student's behaviour, the focus of any discussion. By doing this, they do not create personal barriers, which are sometimes difficult to overcome and which are certainly not conducive to learning.

One of the best ways for a teacher to avoid conflict, maintain authority and obtain the desired behaviours from their students is to offer them choices. Let me give you three typical examples. As we all know, mobile phones are commonplace in schools today. Virtually every student has one. There are obviously many advantages to youngsters' having phones, but they are the bane of most teachers' lives when they start ringing in class, or when students try to make calls or send messages during lessons. Many schools ban them, while others simply demand that the students do not use them during lesson time. The sanctions in my school are straightforward: if a phone rings or students try to make calls, then the phone is to be confiscated. While I agree that persistent offenders should be dealt with firmly and in accordance with the rules, I do feel there is leeway for alternative action. If this happens in my classroom, I simply say something like, 'Lauren, you know what the rules about mobile phones are and you have a choice. You can either switch the phone off and put it in your bag, or you can give it to me and come to collect it at the end of the day'. I have generally found this method to be highly successful. By adopting this approach, I have maintained my authority, reinforced the school rules, and obtained the desired effect of removing the mobile phone from use in the classroom. The important thing to remember is that in this scenario, there has been no stand-off or impasse where the student has felt pushed into a corner. By giving the student a choice, both parties are able to keep their dignity. The same choice-giving method can be applied to students listening to personal stereos, wearing trainers, and so on.

My other example relates to misbehaviour during lessons. Think about a situation where a student's behaviour has overstepped the mark. You have issued several warnings, but these have remained unheeded. At this point, you need to give the student a choice of actions. You could say something like, 'Teresa, you know the rules about distracting others. You are not allowing the people around you to concentrate. I have spoken to you about this before, but as you have ignored my warnings, I am giving you a choice of actions. You can either move to the front of the class, or you can work on your own outside'.

Have you ever been in a situation where a student simply won't obey your instructions? I certainly have. Perhaps you have asked a student to move from one seat to another, or to leave the room, and they have simply refused to budge. It's one of those stand-off situations again, where time seems to stand still, where you feel the eyes of every student focusing on you, and where you think to yourself, one of us has got to back down here. This situation is all about power! Again, giving the student a choice can often diffuse potential conflict, get you both off the hook, and maintain your credibility in front of the other students. You need to adopt a calm and non-aggressive tone of voice, and say something like: 'Fair enough Michael, I can't make you move – in the end that's down to you, but you do have a choice here. Either you move now, or I will have to catch up with you in your free time so that we can discuss it later. What do you think?' Again, in most cases, I obtain the desired outcome. In situations where youngsters have failed to comply with my instructions, I have told them that I will be calling for them when the 'heat has died down'. I have then collected them from their lessons just before the morning or dinner-time break so that I can talk to them in their own time about the issue.

One of the things I focus on in my previous book (*Managing Your Classroom*, 2007), is the issue of students' secondary behaviour. When a teacher gets distracted from the initial disciplinary issue and starts to focus on the subsequent inappropriate behaviour of the student, then conflict is likely to arise. The best way to explain this is to give you a typical example. Teacher A notices Hannah passing a note across the table to Darren when they are supposed to be taking a test under examination conditions. 'Bring the note here please Darren'. The whole class stops work to look at Darren, who grins, stands up and swaggers over to the front of the class. As he walks past Ashley, he playfully hits him on the back of the head. 'Ouch'! shouts Ashley. The rest of the students start laughing. Darren is in his element – a captive audience – great! He then screws the note up and flings it, basketball style, on to the teacher's desk. There is no doubt that Darren's behaviour, subsequent to the note-passing incident, is unacceptable, but there are two ways the teacher can react here. In this first scenario the teacher focuses on Darren's secondary behaviour and challenges him on three counts, even before he tackles the primary cause of his displeasure, that is, the irregular communication during an examination. Teacher A yells at Darren for grinning disrespectfully at him. As a result of this, Darren rolls his eyes and scowls back at him 'God, I was only smiling! There's no law against that is there'? 'Don't be insolent, Darren, or I'll give you a detention'. Then Teacher A reacts angrily when he sees Ashley being hit by Darren. 'Leave Ashley alone, Darren, he's done nothing to you'. 'Yes, he has', says Darren. 'He called me a loser for not being able to do the test.' 'Well, perhaps you are a loser if you someone has to pass you a note with the answer on it!' shouts Teacher A. 'I'm not the loser! – You're the loser, you're really sad'! shouts Darren. The final straw occurs when Darren really 'takes the Mickey' by throwing the paper on to the teacher's desk. 'Right, that's it, Darren! Enough is enough – get out of my room – I will not accept such insolence! Go down to the Head of Year. He can sort you out!'

Ask yourself – who really won in this situation? The working week in a school is absolutely littered with incidents such as these, where teachers become embroiled in the secondary behaviour of students. The mistake that Teacher A made was to focus entirely on Darren's secondary behaviour and to ignore the primary issue. I am not saying that his inappropriate behaviour should not be challenged. However, this could have been done at a later point and in a less aggressive fashion. By doing this, the issue could also have been discussed without an audience. Teacher A needed to focus all his attention on the main issue; that of highlighting the need for students to abide by the regulations set out by examination boards. Earlier in this chapter, I advised you not to push students into a corner. You should also be very careful not to back yourself into a corner where the only outcome is likely to be conflict. I am sure you will agree that in this particular incident Teacher A 'set himself up for a fall'!

Now take time to think about this classroom scenario: break-time has just ended. The teacher is ready to start the lesson. A young lad with a reputation for being 'challenging' brings his football in to the classroom and starts bouncing the ball provocatively on the desk. The teacher walks over to the desk, snatches the ball and takes it to front of the classroom.

Teacher: 'Right, give the ball to me – this isn't the playground'.

Student: 'That's not fair! You haven't started the lesson yet'!

Teacher: 'I don't care – you know you shouldn't have brought the ball into the room'.

Student: 'You can't do that – it's my ball. You've got no right to take it. It's mine'!

Teacher: 'I can do what I like, I'm the teacher'!

Student: 'You're a useless teacher – I hate you'!

Teacher: 'Don't speak to me like that! You need to show some respect!'

Student: 'Why should I respect you? Your lessons are ...:..........'!'
(Student walks out)

Again, this situation is all about power! Both the teacher and the student want the last word. However, it is important not to forget who the adult is. It is the teacher's responsibility to recognize what the student is trying to do, and to deal with the situation in an authoritative, objective and assertive manner. However, in this case, both parties see the situation as a personal battle and all about winning and losing. The student is deliberately trying to deflect the issue away from the original offence – that of bouncing the ball in the classroom. He knows that he was wrong but is upset by the aggressive and autocratic manner in which the teacher has dealt with the issue. He wants to punish the teacher for causing him to lose face in front of his peers. The teacher, on the other hand, has almost forgotten about the original issue and is focusing on the rudeness and disrespect of the student concerned. He feels that his authority has been threatened in front of the other students in the class. Both parties are highly charged emotionally and the situation has reached an impasse!

You will remember that earlier in this chapter, we explored ways in which this type of situation can be prevented through the use of an authoritative teaching style. Let's assume that you have done all you can to adopt this approach; you have given this student choices; you have spoken to them in a polite, calm assertive and authoritative manner; you have not pushed them into a corner but have given them time to comply with your instructions. Unfortunately, although you are confident that you have done everything by the book on this occasion, this just hasn't worked. So, again, where do you go from here? Obviously there is a need to follow things up with this youngster at some point. My advice would be not to deal with the issue there and the, but to say something like. 'I feel we both need a bit of time away from this. I'll have a chat with you at the end of the lesson'. You may even feel that the youngster needs a longer period of time to calm down, and you will have to judge the situation for yourself. However, what is absolutely imperative is that you do come back to the youngster and challenge his/her behaviour.

So far, we have focused on how an authoritative teacher deals with inappropriate student behaviour. However, it is important to remember that there is much more to establishing good working relationships with students than just reacting in an appropriate manner to their misbehaviour. A good teacher will scan the classroom actively looking for those students on task and celebrate student success where relevant. An authoritative teacher has enough self-esteem and feels relaxed enough to make good use of humour in the classroom. Most importantly, a good teacher will not be afraid to show their human side to students. We all get things wrong occasionally and, if you are trying to encourage a high level of reflectivity among your students, it is important to apologize to them when you get it wrong. When I say apologize, I don't mean in a fawning, sycophantic manner – that would simply be seen by many students to be a sign of weakness. Throughout my career, there have been many occasions where I have overreacted to a student's inappropriate behaviour, and where I have been too acerbic or robust in my disciplinary responses. In these situations I try very hard to make amends, by asking to see the student concerned, and by trying to re-establish good relationships with them. I remember doing this with one particular Year Nine student who was really winding me up with some low level, but nevertheless, annoying behaviour. Let's call this student John. I remember the lesson well. I was feeling very tired and stressed and things were going quite badly during the lesson. John was off-task and laughing at one of his friends. Suddenly I simply snapped. I let John have it! John's misdemeanour was trivial and certainly didn't warrant the personal attack I made on him. I felt awful about the situation and knew I had to do something about it. I called John to see me during the afternoon registration session, and apologized for the way that I had spoken to him. I told him that, although his behaviour was unacceptable, I had no right to speak to him like that. John was so taken aback by my apology, that I experienced no further problems with him for the rest of that year. In fact, I would go even further than this by saying that this simple apology improved my relationship with this youngster so dramatically that, a year later, he came to see me to check if 'I was alright'. You will remember me extolling the virtues of Zimpher and Howey who describe the four domains of teaching and the need for teachers to adopt a balanced approach towards their job. I feel that the description of events shown above together with the summary diagram in Figure 2.3 reflects my effective use of the personal domain. Remember that in this domain, the conception of teaching is one of a self-actualized person who uses himself or herself as an effective and humane instrument of classroom instruction.

This teacher focuses on the rights of all students to learn.

This teacher uses the strength

This teacher looks for opportunities to praise and to encourage students and to celebrate their successes.

This teacher uses preventative class management measures to minimize student disruption. (S)he plans these into their lessons.

This teacher uses respectful language to the students even when angry.

This teacher issues instructions clearly and firmly.

This teacher does not verbally attack students, but challenges the inappropriateness of their behaviour.

This teacher knows when to apologize.

This teacher knows when to tactically ignore inappropriate secondary behaviour.

This teacher doesn't hold a grudge and tries to re-establish good working relationships as soon as possible.

Do you recognize any of your behaviours here?

Figure 2.3 Characteristics of a democratic teaching style

I feel that I was successful in showing him a number of things – that teachers get things wrong; that it is not a sign of weakness to apologize; that I was right to criticize his behaviour, but wrong to make a personal attack on him; that relationships can be rebuilt successfully after conflict. Although this was a successful outcome I do not lay claim to getting it right in every situation. But I keep trying.

Hopefully you will have noted from the descriptions of the various teaching styles that you as teachers have what it takes to create within your students what Schindler (2010) calls a 'psychology of success'. Instead of focusing entirely on what is presented before you in your daily professional lives – that is, the students, the physical environment, the culture of the school, I am asking you to adopt a different approach and to consider how your thought process and mindset might impact upon your students' learning. As

Schindler (2010) so aptly puts it, 'the vast majority of our activity each day occurs between our ears. If we are intentional about it, we will be much more effective'. I totally concur with his views that 'what primarily keeps teachers from effectiveness and/or growing into the kinds of professionals that they would like to become is most often found in the domain of their thought processes and habits'. In other words, 'what holds us up is not usually a lack of information or insufficient talent, but our ways of thinking'.

Having explored the characteristics of the autocratic, indecisive and authoritative teacher take a look at the following table and see if you can apply these to the model presented below. You will note that in the Effective Teacher category (see Figure 2.4) the teacher creates a highly democratic classroom culture by providing his/her students with numerous opportunities to make decisions both on an individual and group basis. Having said this, the teacher is able to use his/her good interpersonal skills to create effective learning relationships and clear behaviour boundaries for the lesson. Because students want to please the teacher and because they feel secure enough to take risks and to show positivity, they are comfortable in setting themselves targets and in foregoing gratification; that is, giving up the chance to mess about in class in an attempt to realize their goals. In this scenario the teacher adopts an authoritative approach and is comfortable in using what I call the 'language of inevitability' when setting out his/her behaviour and learning expectations. Students understand why they are doing the work and respond well to the teacher's use of extrinsic and intrinsic motivational strategies. In this scenario the teacher orchestrates the activities and behaviour of the class in the same way a conductor directs the various sections of an orchestra. He/she does not adopt the over-dominant role displayed by the autocratic teacher but uses his/her authority to facilitate learning thus empowering and enabling the students in his/her lessons.

A quick scan of the lower half of the table will provide you with good descriptors of what it is like to be in the classes of autocratic or indecisive teachers. Just as in the class of the indecisive Mr X, the maths teacher described earlier, rules are fluid and students are unsure as to exactly where they stand. Both indecisive and autocratic teachers do not plan to create a positive climate for learning, but they do tend to adopt a reactive stance towards student misbehaviour. As a result of this, students either conform passively, but with little enthusiasm for the work, or they openly rebel and cause further conflict. In these scenarios a lack of thought and planning by the teacher often leads to unclear targets (if any are set at all) being set for the students and a complete lack of motivational input from the teacher. Instead of acting as enabler the autocratic teacher uses his energy to break the will of the students in an attempt to get through the lesson as comfortably as possible. On the other hand, the indecisive teacher affords *too much* attention acquiescing to the whims of his students in an attempt to keep the peace. His classroom management is chaotic and reactive in style and it is extremely easy for many students to slip through the net.

You are right if you are beginning to realize that the basis for all good teaching is relationships. Gilbert (2002 p. 136–137) quite rightly points out that teaching is about relationships. He says that 'once you get these right children will leap through hoops of flame for you. Get them wrong-and it can feel like the other way round'. It is important for you as beginning teachers to recognize that creating a climate for learning is just as much

	Student-Centred	Teacher-Centred
Effective	**1 TEACHER** **Authoritative Teacher** **Facilitator** ● Relationship-driven ● Goal = self-directed students ● Motivation = internal/ build sense of self-efficacy ● Clear boundaries ● Build students' collective responsibility ● Answers 'why we are dong this?' ● Long-term goals (the management may be messy at first, but auto-pilot by end) ● Our class	**2 TEACHER** **Authoritative Teacher** **Orchestrator** ● Structure-driven Goal = on task behaviour ● Motivation = external/ positive reinforcement ● Clear consequences ● Build students' collective efficiency ● Answers 'what is expected?' ● Short-term goals (the management should be in good shape by the second week) ● My Class
Ineffective	**3 TEACHER** **Indecisive Teacher** **Enabler** ● Reaction-driven ● Goal = keep students happy ● Motivation = student interests ● Unclear boundaries ● Students – increasingly self-centred ● Chaotic energy ● Goals are vague (management problems happen early and are still happening by end of the term) ● The students	**4 TEACHER** **Autocratic Teacher** **Dominator** ● Obedience-driven ● Goal = let students know who is boss ● Motivation = to avoid punishment ● Arbitrary punishments ● Students – increasingly immune to coercion ● Negative energy ● Goals is to break students will (students respond out of fear, but slowly increase hostility and rebellion) ● Those students

Figure 2.4 (*Contd.*)

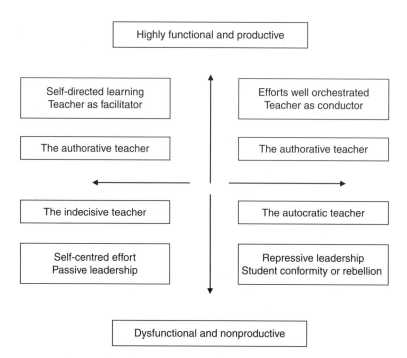

Figure 2.4 Teaching styles and their effectiveness

about improving and developing appropriate teacher behaviour as it is about improving student behaviour. In other words, it is not just students who you have to educate – you, too, may have to change!

It's all an act really!

It must have become pretty obvious by now that, like the animal kingdom, there is a pecking order in the classroom. As Bennett (2010) puts it, 'Issues of dominance, status and self-image are crucial in the classroom context. Why? Because you are going to have to get your pupils to do your bidding and to exert some kind of control over them in order to get any teaching done'. Put quite simply, if you want to be a successful teacher you have got to make sure that you fully understand your need to control others. Having said this, you also need to be aware of the most effective ways to do this. Hopefully, you will have deducted from the descriptions of the authoritative teacher that, despite being courteous, thoughtful, empathic and humorous, these teachers all display what I call 'The Edge'. (Dixie 2007) Students soon learn not to 'mess with them'. In short, these teachers tend to 'say what they mean, and mean what they say' and recognize that 'empty threats are no threats at all'. So, what does this mean in practice? Basically if you warn a student that should they continue to behave in an inappropriate manner, you will have to take action, then you simply need to carry your threats out. Failure to do this will result in your giving the strong message to the student that you are not to be taken seriously, and this will ultimately result in a complete loss of your status.

There is a view that 80 per cent of communication is non-verbal. Whether this is the precise figure or not is irrelevant – what matters is that body language and tone of voice are probably the most powerful tools in the authoritative teacher's toolkit. This is where your acting ability comes in. No matter how lacking in confidence you might be, summon up every ounce of reserve and use a tone of voice and body posture that conveys to the students that you really do mean business. When doing this, ensure that you have a good understanding of your audience. If this is a whole class issue, then scan the classroom and make eye contact with each and every student. The key area to get right is your level of eye contact. Students can see immediately whether you are serious simply by looking at your eyes. If you have any doubts about your ability to do this don't show these. In short, don't bottle it!

When speaking to students, ensure that you use the 'language of inevitability' (Dixie 2011). In other words, speak to the students with assumed authority. You are strongly advised not to 'blow your top' when admonishing students because doing so demonstrates to the students that you are not in control of your emotions and if you can't achieve this level of control, then why should they? Having said this, you may need to raise your voice in order to gain the attention of the class – that's fine, but having done this, bring the pitch of your voice down. Do not garble or rush your words, but speak in a slow and even manner, keeping the pitch of your voice just above conversational level. In the same way that you would rehearse for drama production, practise this at home.

You will have noticed that the most authoritative teachers 'walk tall'. Adopt a central position in the classroom – do not move around the room otherwise the more motoric of students will focus on your movement rather than on your words. Place your feet firmly on the ground, keep your head up, put your hands down by your sides and hold your ground.

In the same way that an animal establishes its territory, you need to establish that the classroom is your territory. As a teacher you have the right to change the seating arrangements as often as you want to do. It's your space so let the students know this – do not let them run the agenda.

So what have we discovered so far in this chapter? We have continued our exploration of the work of Zimpher and Howey, who suggest that a teacher's role should comprize of four domains: the technical, the clinical, the personal and the critical. I have shown my support for their view, that a good teacher should maintain a balance between all four domains and that he/she should not be over-reliant on any specific one. We have also ascertained that there are teachers with varying degrees of self-esteem and that the level of a teacher's self-worth can seriously impact on the quality of their teacher–student relationships. We have also discussed Lewin's classification of the three different types of teachers, and have explored the implications of teaching and management styles on teacher-student relationships. In addition to this, we have looked at the effect of these relationships on the culture of learning in the classroom. Finally, we have briefly explored the significance of creating 'achieved' status through positive use of body language, voice tone and eye contact as a means of aspiring to become an authoritative teacher.

Throughout this chapter, I have asked you, implicitly and, sometimes explicitly, to think about your own sense of self-worth and how this may have affected your own teaching style. I have also asked you to consider where you might place yourself along this teaching/ management-style continuum. However, I am fully aware that, at this point of your career, this may be easier said than done. Adopting this high level of reflectivity is not only intellectually demanding, but is also time-consuming and physically and emotionally exhausting. The process also requires a level of confidence and self-esteem not usually found among teachers in their first few years of teaching. Nevertheless, my advice to you is to start your reflective journey now and to simply do what you can under the circumstances. However, do not expect to get things completely right first time! You need to know that this would be a tall order for even the most experienced and reflective of teachers. Although my confidence levels and professional sense of worth are pretty high, these have fluctuated quite dramatically at times during the academic year. You may be surprised to know that I am not alone in feeling like this. I give a lot of attention in my book *Managing Your Classroom* (2007) to the importance of a teacher's emotional state of mind and confidence levels when starting with their new classes in September. The following quotes from two very experienced teachers show that no matter how long we have been teaching, we all experience peaks and troughs in our emotional state and confidence levels. This response comes from a very capable and highly respected assistant HOD with 24 years of experience:

> The night before we return in September I know I am going to sleep badly. I wake up every hour and get up very early even though I know I have got everything ready the night before. I have to force myself to eat and drink as I always feel sick. Once I am at school I feel even sicker. When my classes arrive my mouth goes dry – I never sit down for the first lessons. I suppose I need to look more menacing and, as I am only small, standing when they are sitting seems to make a difference. I go over what they do when arriving to the lesson, what equipment I expect them to have and my expectations of how they should behave and so on. I try to get them to give me reasons for rules. and I probably talk for too long! I've had nightmares about arriving a day late for school and about my classes having no teacher for that first day! At the end of the first day I am truly exhausted. I've used up my nervous energy for the next month in one go. (Dixie 2007)

This next response comes from an extremely efficient and well-respected senior teacher with 25 years' experience who was, nevertheless, still prepared to expose her vulnerabilities in writing.

> I always feel really nervous before the first day in September. I never sleep well the night before and I don't feel confident when the day arrives (after 25 years). I always try to stand in the foyer early in the morning to meet the students as they arrive just to get into the swing of things! When I meet my classes for the first time I feel nervous and unsure of myself. I always go through my routines and what is expected of them but I always try to get a bit of maths in there too so that I get to know their names as soon as possible. Something they can succeed at – nothing too difficult – so that they can go away and look forward to coming back. (Dixie 2007)

The reason I have included these two extracts is to show you that the feelings and emotions you may currently be experiencing do not go away completely. As you get more experienced, you learn to accept and deal with these and move on. Bearing in mind that you, as beginning teachers, are still learning the trade and do not have the same cushion of experience to fall back on, you are more likely to experience emotional extremes. I have spoken to many beginning teachers who have felt absolute elation and despair, all within the same lesson! There is also no doubt that a teacher's emotional state can have direct consequences on the way they relate to their students. As we have already discussed, teachers with a lack of confidence tend to be irritable, to snap at youngsters and to over-react to incidents that occur in their classrooms. On the occasions when this has happened to me, I have apologized to the student(s) concerned, explained to them that I am 'having a bad day' and asked them to be understanding of my situation. I have to say that this only works if you do the same for them, when they too are struggling with their self-esteem and confidence levels.

So how do you become the type of teacher you aspire to be? How do you become more confident? How do you learn to control your emotional state? My response to these questions is quite simple: with an open mind, a willingness to celebrate your own strengths, an acceptance of your own shortcomings and a great deal of effort! I also advise beginning teachers to keep a reflective journal in which they can record their feelings, emotions, and the events that have occurred within their working week. Keeping a journal during the initial stages of your teaching career can help you to learn from your experiences, and can serve to show you how far you have really come during your time in the school. If you aspire to be the authoritative practitioner described earlier in this chapter, you need to develop your reflective practice as means of establishing and maintaining good quality learning relationships with your students.

According to Schön (1983), reflective practice is the process of thoughtfully considering one's own experiences in applying knowledge to practice while being coached by professionals in the discipline. In education, it refers to the process of the educator studying his/her own teaching methods and determining what works best for the students. Schön emphasizes that teachers have to cope with the fact that no two groups of students are alike and that even with students with whom they are familiar, they constantly have to present new material to them. This inevitably creates its own unique problems in terms of explanation and understanding. The teacher has to constantly reflect upon, and react to, the ever-changing scenarios that occur in his/her classroom in such a way that the process appears to be seamless to the students. He termed this process 'reflection-*in*-action'. In new situations, the practitioner is able to bring certain aspects of his/her work to his/her level of consciousness, reflect upon it and reshape it without interrupting the flow of proceedings. For those of you who are experienced teachers you probably do this quite naturally and intuitively, without giving the process a great deal of thought. However, to those teachers in the dawn of their careers, this process does not come naturally and it is highly likely that you become somewhat flustered when new scenarios are presented to you and in situations when things don't quite go according to plan. My message to you as beginning teachers is not to worry too much about this at the moment – things will get better with experience. Some of the unpredictable and untoward things that are likely to throw you off track in the initial stages of your teaching will be of little or no consequence as you become more used to the role.

Reflection-*in*-action largely involves 'situated knowledge' and is a process that we often go through without necessarily being able to say exactly what we are doing. Reflecting on, and articulating our thoughts about our teaching *after* the lesson has happened, is called 'reflection-*on*-action'. I am in total agreement with Schön who believed passionately that reflection-*on*-action is a key process in learning how to teach. In Schön (1983), he argues that no matter how inadequate a beginning teacher's verbal reconstruction of events, it is only by constantly bringing the ways in which they are framing their teaching situations to their level of consciousness, that they will eventually gain control of their own teaching. The following quote from Schön (1987) cited in Furlong and Maynard (1995), makes the point clearly.

> As I think back on my experience . . . I may consolidate my understanding of the problem or invent a better or more general solution to it. If I do, my present reflection on my earlier reflection-in-action begins a dialogue of thinking and doing through which I become more skilful.

All ITT providers will encourage reflection-*in*-action and will highlight this as an area for development in your classroom practice. They will also insist that some kind of reflection-*on*-action takes place in the form of a reflective journal or series of lesson evaluations. Using this 'reflection-*on*-action' process as a model I have worked with a colleague to create a reflective formula which is currently used by trainees in two ITT programmes. I have presented the general principles underlying the formula in Figure 2.4 and have also provided four extracts from the reflective logs of some of my trainees. In order to support the diagram presented in Figure 2.4, I will briefly take you through the process as described in the formula.

You are first required simply to *describe* the professional scenario presented to you. This could be something that happened in the classroom, an incident in the school corridor or your observations of interactions between colleagues and/or students. At this point in the reflective process, there is no evaluative input whatsoever – you merely need to describe the scenario. Having done this, you now need to describe the perceived consequences of what you have just experienced; in other words, what happened because of what happened. For example, you may have noticed that in one of your lesson observations that a science teacher failed to establish his/her expectations, rules and sanctions before he/she allowed the students to carry out an experiment. The consequences of him/her not doing this might have been that the students behaved in an unruly fashion thus disrupting learning in the lesson. Another consequence could be that laboratory health and safety rules were breached and an accident occurred. I call these crucial decision-making factors in a lesson 'watershed moments' because they represent specific points in lessons where teachers' actions or inactions can lead to varying and sometimes adverse consequences (Dixie, 2007). As part of the induction process in my school, I asked trainees to carry out lesson observations that require them to identify these watershed moments in lessons, and to then describe the subsequent consequences arising from these. You will also note from the diagram that this is also the place to describe your emotional responses to the scenarios presented to you. In Dixie (2007) I give a high profile to the importance of exploring the emotional side of teaching. I feel strongly that recognizing and dealing with your emotional responses to teaching is an important part of the reflective process.

Experience shows me that most beginning teachers are quite adept at describing professional scenarios but are far less skilled at recognizing watershed moments and/or the potential consequences of them. In most cases, this is where their reflective practice usually ends. Unless pressurized, most beginning teachers do not take the process any further. They neither identify the implications of their teaching experiences nor do they show how they have modified or altered their practice in the light of their reflections. If the reflective cycle illustrated in Figure 2.4 is to be successfully realized then the third and fourth requirements need to be fulfilled. Having responded to your reflections by taking the appropriate action, the whole reflective process starts over again. This document does not have to be completed electronically nor does it have to be completed in the column form presented in Figure 2.5. It is, however, very important that the criteria in all four stages are met if you want to demonstrate your skill as a reflective practitioner and realize the standards presented in Figure 2.6.

Identification/description of professional scenarios.	What are the perceived consequences of these behaviours?	What are the implications and targets for your professional practice?	What evidence do you have to show how you have used this experience to develop your professional practice?
In a Year Eight lesson I had planned. I had arranged a starter activity which involved a ball.

The objective was to introduce naturaliztic performance and students would have to throw the ball to another student whilst acting an emotion so essentially the ball became a transfer of emotion from one student to the next.

In this particular lesson I trusted that the students would do this sensibly and did not feel the need to issue health and safety instructions.

When the group started the activity several of the boys in the group took it upon themselves to hurl the ball with no real thinking at another student. The starter activity was carried out whilst I was writing the learning objective on the board. | As I was writing the learning objective several of the boys saw this as an ideal opportunity to throw the ball as hard as they could at walls and other students. As I had not explained and trusted that the students would behave in a safe manner, I gave them the go ahead to behave inappropriately.

One student was hit in the face by the ball and the point of the starter was not achieved as the students saw this as a simple throwing and catching exercise. | Doing this kind of starter activity again, I would make sure that I was organized by giving the students a settler task whilst writing the learning objective rather than allowing them to conduct the starter activity with my back turned. This was bad organization on my part as had I have been supervising the activity the students would have gained a lot more from it from a learning perspective.

Trusting that students would behave sensibly was another mistake on my part. As the majority of students do know how to behave in drama, but having a ball somehow made it seem more like a PE lesson. The ball was a new experience in the lesson and one of which I should have explained how to behave appropriately. By not giving the students my expectations of the exercise, it resulted in them conducting it in an unsafe manner, whilst not benefiting them from an educational point of view. | **How do you know whether you have been successful?**

I have since tried this activity again where I gave a series of instructions, explained rules and expectations. I had fully prepared the lesson in advance so there was no need for me to fuss about at the beginning of the lesson.

The starter activity was this time successful in the sense that it served its purpose of introducing naturalizm via a kinaesthetic approach. |

Figure 2.5 Extract from reflective journal

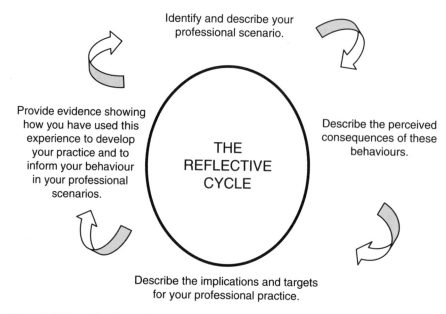

Figure 2.6 The reflective cycle

You are also advised to find a 'critical friend' with whom you can be totally honest in sharing your thoughts, feelings and emotions. If you are fortunate enough, this person could turn out to be your mentor, but this does not necessarily have to be the case. The kind of person you need to confide in is someone who is non-judgemental, who has a full grasp of the reflective process and someone who fully understands the link between a teacher's self-esteem and the quality of their relationships with students. That important 'someone' needs to have an understanding of the qualities of an authoritative teaching style.

Teach with authority

Aspire to be an authoritative teacher. Authoritative teachers:

- have high professional esteem
- are able to use their acting skills to dominate their teaching space
- recognize the value of good relationships with their students
- don't hold grudges or personalize issues.

- can admit when they are wrong
- can empathize with students
- do all they can to enable and empower their students
- are reflective practitioners
- understand and cope effectively with their own emotions
- provide their students with clear boundaries for behaviour.

Suggestions

- Develop the actor in you
- Practise dominating your teaching space in front of the mirror at home
- Produce a script on an index card so that you don't stumble over your words when speaking to the class. Empower yourself by telling the students that because what you have got to say is **so** important, and because you want to make sure that they 'get the message', you've written things down
- Ask members of the Drama Department to coach you in using assertive body language
- Ask experienced teachers to observe you with this focus in mind

3

What do they think of us? – Gaining a student perspective

It is fair to say that, in the distant past, the teacher–student relationship equation was straightforward. The teacher was there to teach – to pass on knowledge, and the student was there to learn – to be the passive recipient of that knowledge. Generally speaking, there was limited interaction between the two parties.

Since the 1980s, however, schools have changed significantly in their attempts to reflect the changing values of society and today, there is a strong feeling that education has become far more 'market-orientated', or client-based, in its function. Manifestations of this can be seen in such governmental initiatives as open enrolment, league tables, and the reorganizing of the Office for Standards in Education, Children's Services and Skills (OFSTED) inspections. The growth of student-centred learning in modern primary and secondary schools means that individual student needs have now become a far more important factor in the educational equation. In an attempt to cope with this sea change, many teachers have had to reappraise their attitudes and roles. The responsibilities of newly qualified teachers today, for example, require them to display a whole gamut of skills such as coordination, monitoring, negotiation, group structuring and resource and personnel management. Obviously, in order to be able to meet these requirements, the teacher has to be able to display certain characteristics sympathetic to this method of working, and also to the increasing amount of student–teacher interaction required in the modern day classroom. It is the premise of this chapter, therefore, that knowledge of students' perceptions of what makes a good teacher will therefore help teachers in their everyday practice. Such knowledge will give teachers a clearer picture of student expectations and help to guide their teaching behaviours in the classroom.

'Hang on a minute', I hear you say. 'I am not here to pander to the needs of my students. Schools should not be likened to superstores, where people can simply walk in and pick and choose what they want off the shelf. Of course, I will do my best to interest and stimulate the students, but I am here to teach, and they will simply have to take it or leave it'. I am afraid that my reply to this view is quite robust. The reality of the situation in most schools today is that, unless you do take the needs of the students fully into consideration, instead of taking it, your students *will* simply leave it.

As we have mentioned on numerous occasions, good teacher–student relationships lie at the very heart of successful teaching. Good teachers show awareness and an understanding of the interactions between them and their students. Good teachers listen to what their students have to say and to what they want. This doesn't mean to say that they are constantly acquiescing to the whims or demands of these youngsters, but they do listen and, where possible, they do modify their teaching behaviours accordingly. Understanding the 'how', 'what' and 'why' of the way students think helps us to interact positively with them in the classroom. Some time ago I came across an unpublished paper by Kutnik and Jules (1988) which put this notion extremely succinctly: 'Knowledge of students' perceptions therefore, allows others into the world of students' realities – realities which are frequently the source of their beliefs and in turn their behaviours' (Kutnik and Jules 1988).

It is interesting to note that even as far back as the early twentieth century there were some enlightened educational pioneers who explored the importance of understanding the interactive nature of the classroom. These words offered by James Ward, 1926, cited in Taylor (1962), provide the core tenet of this chapter: 'Surely one of the first steps towards the understanding of the young is to know how they regard us.'

So where does this leave you as a beginning teacher? What do you need to do to find out about the perceptions of the students in your classes? To help you to do this, allow me to describe a piece of low-level research I carried out about fifteen years ago.

The preliminary research I carried out provided ample evidence to suggest strongly that the personality characteristics of the teacher make a considerable difference to student behaviour, motivation and achievement. I wanted to look at these teacher characteristics from the perspectives of their students, and to find out exactly how these affected student behaviour and educational output. I decided to use two main research methods. The first involved a free-response essay exercise in which Year Eight students were simply asked to describe the characteristics of their favourite teachers. The responses were analysed using content analysis. The second method took on a more quantitative stance, and involved using a Likert-style questionnaire that was designed to find a correlation between the students' perceptions of their teachers and the amount of effort they made in lessons. For the purposes of this chapter, however, I am going to focus on the students' essay responses because it is predominantly these findings that had such a great influence on my teaching behaviour.

Although I do not feel that it is necessary to further explore the rationale or methodology of this research in any great detail, I do need to include just one piece of additional information. In the initial stages of the research, the students from this specific subject group and I spent some time negotiating a common view of the following teacher characteristics:

- conscientiousness
- enthusiasm
- friendliness
- confidence
- humour
- sensitivity

It was important for us to do this in order that every student had a similar understanding of what these various teacher characteristics meant. I focused on these specific qualities as they represented the main teacher characteristics described in my background reading. Allow me to share the views of a few of these students of their teachers.

Conscientiousness came highest on the list of preferred teacher qualities. Comments relating to a teacher's conscientiousness included references to the teacher being prepared to explain tasks in detail, and using strategies tapered to meet all students' needs. A number of students felt that it was important that the teacher stay in the classroom and not disappear for any length of time. They felt that continued teacher absence from the classroom was extremely demotivating. A number of students felt that teachers should make strenuous efforts to make sure that their students recorded their homework tasks, and that their work should be marked on a regular basis. Failure to do so, they said, would result in poor student effort when completing subsequent assignments. One student put his case quite vehemently: 'When you've got homework and you've tried your best, you want to get it marked don't you? This is an important thing you must do.'

Another student actually quantified the exact amount of homework a student of at this age should do, quoting extracts from the school's homework policy. This was supported by another student, who stated that:

> The teacher should take the books in on a regular basis so that all marking is kept up to date. For example, teacher X may take students' books in and keep marking up to date, so if there are students who are having difficulties, these problems can be sorted out. Teacher Y may hardly ever take books in to mark so some students who are struggling may never be helped unless they have the courage to ask.

A substantial number of students mentioned that a good teacher is thoroughly prepared for lessons, with as many external stimuli as possible (i.e. videos, audio tapes, PowerPoint slides, etc.). One student said about this: "I think a teacher who has given a lot of thought to the lesson and knows what he/she is going to say or do makes a lesson go more smoothly."

Some of the students wrote about the importance of the teacher insisting upon a good standard of work. One student in particular said about this issue: 'If a student's work is messy then I think that the teacher who is teaching should make them do it again. If the student hasn't done their work then I think the teacher should give them a detention'. It seemed clear from the very high number of times students mentioned some aspect of conscientiousness that this characteristic features very highly in a student's expectations of a good teacher. My secondary research confirmed that there was a direct link between the conscientiousness of teachers and the work rate, performance and behaviour of their students.

As was the case with the adults referred to in Chapter One, many students referred to the importance of teacher enthusiasm in the learning equation, making statements such as: 'If a teacher is enthusiastic about his/her subject, this enthusiasm will often rub off on their students' and 'he/she will encourage me to work hard and be enthusiastic about ideas that I discuss with them'. One specific student took this idea further by explaining what he actually meant by the term 'enthusiastic' behaviour:

> A teacher should have different tones of voice to make things exciting and also interesting, so you don't fall asleep with boredom in the class. My English teacher from Year Seven sounded exciting when explaining a piece of work and also when reading to the class.

Another student, when talking about the importance of making eye contact as part of the repertoire of an enthusiastic teacher, carried on to describe the teaching behaviour of a particular teacher: 'The way she conducted the lesson with such ease but so much enthusiasm and she looked her eyes with everyone's and walked in between our desks involving all students.'

Although many of the comments about teacher enthusiasm were not as well developed as those for teacher conscientiousness, the importance of enthusiasm could be inferred from the very context of these comments. Throwaway lines, such as 'a teacher should be enthusiastic and make the work sound good and not boring', were common.

What certainly emerged from this exercise was the importance of teacher warmth and friendliness. One student talked about this in some detail:

> Another important quality in a teacher is friendliness. If a teacher is friendly towards their students, the students will feel more inclined to talk to the teacher if they have a personal problem or, if they do not understand the work they have been set.

Often associated with their descriptions of a 'friendly' teacher was 'cheerfulness', and the two qualities were often taken as synonymous. One student wrote about the importance of friendliness but went on to say that this, in itself, was not enough. They expected the teacher to be friendly but 'firm', so that real learning could take place in a relaxed atmosphere.

It also seemed to be extremely important to the students that teachers made them feel welcome when they entered the classroom. One student took this a stage further by describing the type of teacher behaviour that made him/her feel welcome:

> Another thing I find welcoming in the lesson is when your teacher speaks your language like "Hi! – you alright?" and things like that. That makes the lesson feel more comfortable because you know that he/she is stooping? down to your level just to make you feel welcome.

Again, the secondary data used in this study supported the essence of this primary research.

Classifying teacher 'confidence' was quite difficult. Where students had not specifically mentioned this term, I had to infer its importance from their descriptions of what I saw to be the behaviour of a confident teacher in terms of class control and in dealing firmly but fairly with students. Comments such as the one shown below help to exemplify my point:

> Teachers should always maintain a good level of discipline with students in the class. This is important because you know the teacher is in charge but you can still have a laugh and it does not get out of hand.

A number of students took this line; some went on to mention that if this firmness is not achieved in the classroom, then little or no work will be carried out. Some students went on to mention overtly about the importance of confidence and how a lack of confidence, often displayed by inexperienced teachers, can often lead to a breakdown in discipline and disrupt learning.

As expected, a sense of humour was extremely important to students. They felt that a teacher's ability to display a good sense of humour made the atmosphere in the class a 'happy one'. One student referred to the importance of the teacher being able to take a joke, and stressed the importance of the teacher being 'funny'. He went on to say: 'I do not mean joke telling. I mean saying something funny on the spur of the moment or "taking the 'Micky" out of someone; e.g. a slide of an old car and saying it is a particular teacher's car.' One student, when talking about humour and teachers who motivate him, said: 'I hate boring teachers – that just makes me bored and so I don't listen and so I don't do any work.'

The term 'teacher sensitivity' can cover a multitude of behaviours. For the purpose of this exercise, it was taken to mean an obvious sympathy for the individual student's physical, emotional, social and mental well-being. An element of caring was therefore involved here. One student, when writing about the importance of a teacher caring about his/her students, stated: 'I feel this is important because each student needs to feel they are important. Each student has different abilities, and a caring teacher will always consider this and give positive criticizms to these students.' Many students wrote about how important it was for the teacher to be sympathetic to those in difficulty, as well as the necessity for teachers to listen to students' problems. Real learning, they say, cannot take place if students are unhappy.

What immediately became obvious when I began analysing the responses to the student questionnaires was how sophisticated many of these were, and how astute the observations of these young people were of our performances in the classroom. The question that needed asking, however, was whether older children hold similar views of their teachers. It was with precisely this question in mind that I carried out a survey of student perceptions of good teachers with a hundred Year Ten and Year Eleven students. The reason behind doing this was to ascertain whether those extra few years made any difference in terms of their views on teaching behaviours. What immediately became evident was that the majority of these older students recognized the fine balance that teachers need to strike between showing humour, warmth, care and concern, and maintaining good order in their classrooms.

The findings of this research showed me that teachers' ability to control their classes became an increasingly dominant pre-requisite as these youngsters moved into adolescence. Here are some of the older students' views:

> Teacher 'X' is a strict teacher but is very good as he makes us learn. They have a good personality and you can get along with them.

> Teacher 'X' keeps the class under control and makes the lesson interesting and doesn't make the class bored.

> This teacher is strict and keeps his students under control without fail. If he is in a good mood, you will have a fun lesson and enjoy it. This teacher is respected by all, not because he is strict, but because he has earned it.

> A good teacher is someone who can keep a class under control and makes the work interesting. I think that they have a sense of humour, is someone who listens, who helps you to understand things better. Every teacher must have rules but not be too strict.

> Teacher 'X' has a good personality who has his own rules. These rules are not too harsh. They are not strict but can keep the class under control. Their lesson is ready and well prepared for when you basically walk into the classroom.

> I think a good teacher is someone who is strict but also has a laugh with you every now and again. You know they actually want to teach you and that they are always positive and help you when you are stuck.

> Teacher 'X' is good teacher because they are not afraid to send out any trouble-makers so that the rest of the class can work. They also joke about with the class so that the students can have a nice

working environment. Teacher 'X' can get serious with the class and make them work in silence but normally they will let us talk during the lesson. Overall, teacher 'X' is humorous and is a good laugh.

A sense of humour and teacher warmth continue to be important pre-requisites of a good teacher, but *only* when combined with the ability to control the class. About 95 per cent of the older respondents mentioned the teacher's need to have a sense of humour and to be able to 'have a laugh' with their students:

> Teacher 'X' is a very good teacher for two reasons. They manage to keep control of their classes but still maintain a good sense of humour. They like to have a good laugh and joke.
>
> A good teacher has a laugh with the class but we still learn things.
>
> A good teacher has a lot of charisma and a good sense of humour.

However, it is not as straightforward as this. I mentioned earlier that the older students were able to recognize the need for their teachers to take a balanced approach. The following two comments by Year Eleven students exemplify this:

> A bad teacher tries to be funny but simply isn't.
>
> A good teacher doesn't always have to be the centre of attention.

What was also particularly interesting about these findings was that, as the students move into adolescence, they identify good teachers as being good listeners and being there for them to talk to. We need to remember that this is a particularly traumatic time for many young people, and we should never underestimate their need for many of them to talk to adults other than their parents.

> Teacher 'X' is an excellent teacher because he is a very reliable, kind and valuable teacher to have around. The respect I have for him is like no other teacher I have had. I have learned so much from him and he is always around for me to talk to and I know he will help me with any problem.
>
> Teacher 'X' is an excellent teacher. She is well-respected and kind and helps a lot. She is always there for helpful advice. She is more like a friend than a teacher. She is one of us!

However, kindness and consideration do not seem to be enough for many students as they move up into their examination years. For example, many students described some of their teachers as being kind, but then went on to mention how ineffective they were in the classroom. The following comments from two Year Eleven students get this point across well.

> Teacher 'X' is a kind teacher but goes through things too fast for me to understand the information properly.
>
> Teacher 'X' is O.K. but needs to control the class more. She waits too long and students get bored and mess about … Teacher 'X' is a nice teacher but needs to be in control of what the class are doing and to set work to do so that they get stuck into it. Teacher 'X' needs to set something interesting so that the class don't become a nuisance.

You will understand when reading Chapter Five that, as many children move into their teens, their boredom threshold is likely to become significantly lower. My research showed that while these students also wanted their teachers to be firm, fair and fun, they were also a lot more demanding when it came to the teaching styles employed. In addition to the six traits described earlier, many older students made comments that related to teaching and learning issues: Will the teacher be able and willing to explain things to us clearly? Will they make themselves accessible when we are experiencing difficulties? How well can teachers introduce a variety of teaching and learning styles? Will they have a good fund of subject knowledge? The following student comments provide a flavour of these views:

> Teacher 'W' is a good teacher because in class you are able to do presentations, i.e. radio, video and PowerPoint presentations. You can also do posters and leaflets and this helps us learn because it is more interesting and is easier to learn and to remember things.
>
> Teacher 'W' is also a good teacher because at the beginning of each lesson we do a starter activity and so we are prepared for the lesson ahead. Teacher 'W' also has a scheme to motivate students. This scheme is the 'student of the month' where a certificate and a postcard are awarded and sent home. This helps to motivate me and everybody else because the want to win the award.
>
> Teacher 'W' is also a good teacher because they are not only a good speaker and teacher, but a good listener, friend. Teacher 'W' is a

good teacher because you can have a laugh and talk but you do also have to work.

Teacher 'X' motivates their students by spending his own money on prizes for project winners.

To help students he lets them have his own personal details so that they can contact him to receive help whenever they need it. By doing this, they have no excuse for late homework. He also gives up his own time if students miss lessons.

When he teaches he tries different methods like book methods, group learning and individual projects. He goes over the work again and again until people understand it.

A good teacher has a wide subject knowledge and knows how to present it and to keep students interested and not to lose their concentration

A good teacher knows what they are talking about.

If you are ever stuck he will go over and over it again until you understand. He will listen and explain if you need it. I have never understood this subject so much!

A good teacher is someone who doesn't make us bored but who can make the work enjoyable.

A good teacher has a 'fun' teaching technique.

A good teacher helps us to learn in 'fun' ways.

Now, where have you heard all of this before? Yes, you are absolutely right – the descriptions of the characteristics of good teachers offered by these youngsters, match up perfectly with the description of the authoritative teacher in the previous chapter. So much for the view that teachers shouldn't pander to the whims of their students! These students are not asking for anything that is going to radically threaten the British educational system. They have been honest enough to recognize that their behaviour needs to be controlled, that most of them need and want to learn, and that there should be mutual respect in the classroom. It must also be pretty obvious from what you have read in this chapter that students really are excellent judges of what makes a good teacher. This view is replicated in schools across the UK which put students on their selection panels when appointing new staff, from NQTs right through to head teachers. The following poem written by students and published in the Times Educational Supplement (TES) demonstrates how perceptive students are about their teachers.

> **WANTED!**
> **My Perfect Teacher**
> The perfect teacher holds all these things
> We learn in our lessons from the qualities they bring
> First, they should be understanding and know our names
> They'd mark our books regularly and set us new aims
> We shouldn't spend all lesson sitting in our seats
> There are other ways of learning than reading off sheets
> They need to be strong, firm and fair
> Know us individually and truly care
> But always remember it's OK to have fun
> We laugh too, throw in the odd pun
> They must have control, you can't learn in a zoo
> We need help and structure the whole way through
> So there's the perfect teacher wrapped up in one
> Be loving, caring, strict but still fun!

My message to you as beginning teachers is simple; when you feel secure enough, and providing you take care in setting up the context and rules for your research, you need to spend some time canvassing the opinions of your students about what goes on in your classroom. I should warn you, however, that you need to be very clear about what you are trying to find out. You should not use your findings primarily as a measure of your popularity, but you should take this opportunity to find out about the quality of your teaching and of your professional relationships with your students. While lesson-observation feedback from your colleagues can provide you with a useful 'snapshot' of your teaching, your students also see you when you are off your guard, and on a far more regular basis. They are, therefore, able to give you a broader and more honest perspective on your strengths and weaknesses.

So, how do you go about finding out about the perceptions of your students of the quality of your teaching? As I write, it would be easy for me to walk into my study, take one of my student perception questionnaires off the shelf, and simply replicate it the manuscript. However, this would be neither fair nor helpful to you. I felt secure enough with my classes to be able to take risks, and to ask some quite searching questions of my students. I have known instinctively when things have been going badly and when they have been going reasonably well. Even I found the use of student questionnaires invaluable in providing information that helped me to fine tune and hone my teaching. Although I fully recommend the use of teaching and learning questionnaires with students, I advise you to do so with caution.

Unless you want to open a few wounds, as a beginning teacher, you are going to have to be quite cautious and circumspect in your enquiries. Figure 3.1 provides an example of some questionnaire research carried out by a graduate teacher trainee in the second term of his placement at my secondary school. When reading through his questionnaire, you will see how careful he has been in his use of language. He encourages his students to be constructive and objective in their comments, and in doing so, has reduced the likelihood that they will make insulting or negative personal remarks. You will also notice how he has depersonalized the process, by focusing the students' attention on a number of issues relating to a specific unit of work, rather than solely on his teaching style. True, in a subtle and roundabout way, he has solicited their opinions of his teaching, but he has done this within a wider context of the learning and teaching issues associated with this unit of work. It is also pleasing to see that the questionnaire is by no means a one-way process. There are ample opportunities for the students to be reflective about their own performances and contributions.

Figure 3.1 World War 1 (WW1) Evaluation sheet

1. Read the statements and tick the relevant box.

	Strongly Agree	Agree	Undecided	Disagree	Strongly Disagree
I always work to the best of my ability in class					
I can be distracted in class					
I sometimes distract other people in class					
I listen to instructions carefully					

I always finish tasks set in class in the lesson					
My work is always presented to the best of my ability					
I always title and date my work					
Worksheets are always stuck into my book and labelled					
I always contribute to class discussions and attempt to answer questions					
If I am unclear I always ask for help					

2. Set two targets to improve your work/effort next term:
A. _____
B. _____
3. What elements of the course have you enjoyed? Why? _____
4. What part of the course have you not enjoyed? Why? _____
5. Are there any topics that you would have liked to have studied which we did not study in depth (e.g. Battles, Technology, Shell Shock, Women at War, Eastern Front, Poetry, Aircraft, etc.)?
6. Read the statements and tick the relevant box:

	Strongly Agree	Agree	Undecided	Disagree	Strongly Disagree
The teacher explained tasks clearly					
The teacher explained key terms and incidents clearly and in a way that was easy to understand					

The teacher always gave guidance when it was required					
When marking books the teacher's feedback was helpful					
Tasks set were interesting and improved your understanding of the Great War					

7. What activities would you like to see in lessons that would improve your enjoyment and motivation in Humanities? Please tick appropriate selections and explain.

More debates:
More role play:
More stimulating activities such as videos, games, quizzes:
More individual research:
More group work:
Other:

Using surveys such as the one shown in Figure 3.1 is important for two reasons. They can furnish us with information about our teaching behaviours and about the quality of our lessons. In doing so, they can help us to make informed decisions about our practice. The second and equally important reason is that the process of answering the questions can really help to increase student ownership of their learning. Students appreciate being listened to. The young graduate teacher described how both his standard of teaching and the quality of his relationships with the students in this potentially challenging class improved dramatically in the period after he had carried out this exercise. You do need to be aware, however, that there is a big risk involved in carrying out an enquiry such as this. No matter how hard you try to get the students to be constructive in their comments, you must always be prepared to hear things you do not particularly want to hear. I felt this young man to be extremely brave in carrying out this survey at such an early stage in his teaching career. I am sure that many beginning teachers would, understandably, be a little more reluctant to ask such searching questions.

Difficult as it is, it is imperative that we do ask these types of questions if we want to improve the learning scenarios for our students. The accepted view of teaching is that success in the classroom depends greatly on the quality of teacher–student interaction. Sometimes harmonious interaction occurs naturally when our characteristics or personality traits coincide with the specific requirements of the students. At other times, modification of styles, behaviour and characteristics needs to occur. Students are less likely to modify their behaviour than teachers because (a) they are usually less capable of doing so and (b) because they see it as the teacher's task to motivate them. The crucial questions are, therefore, how far can teachers be trained in effective interaction and how far is it a function of their temperament?

It is fair to say that teachers with certain personality traits will find it easier to adopt a variety of interactional techniques and to identify the cues that make certain styles and characteristics desirable. Other teachers will find this more difficult. This chapter has looked specifically at certain teacher characteristics and their effect on the learning process. It is important to say that a good teacher is not a good teacher simply because she has certain characteristics, but because of that indefinable something that comes into play when the characteristics of that teacher coincide with what is wanted by a particular student at that particular time.

What, then, are the implications of this chapter for you as beginning teachers? If one accepts the premise that the characteristics of a teacher can affect student motivation, then there is obviously a need for action. The importance of inter-relational skills should be stressed in all ITT induction programmes and greater emphasis should be placed on the role of students as a resource for research into classroom practice. Those of you who are still in your NQT induction or training years, need to be proactive in seeking opportunities to involve your students in action-research projects, such as the one described in this chapter. If it is not possible to get involved in grand schemes such as these, simply take opportunities on an everyday basis to talk to your students, and to discover their perceptions of the way things are going in your lessons. One of the things you could do on a regular basis is to hold class meetings to discuss the way things are going and to allow students to air their grievances in an acceptable forum. You could do this by using Circle Time. Simply move the desks to the outer edges of the classroom and position the chairs in a circle around your own chair. As with any lesson activity, you need to launch a clear set of parameters for the discussion. I provided you with examples of these in the list that follows. Having reflected on students' views and opinions, you then can decide whether you need to your teaching behaviours in any way. Our Rules for Circle Time:

- do not interrupt each other;
- signal if you wish to speak;

- do not use put-downs (either verbal or nonverbal) towards each other;
- if you do not wish to speak say 'pass';
- if you chose not to speak, you will be given a second opportunity;
- do not name anyone in a negative way. Instead say, 'Someone constantly takes my equipment', or 'Some people push into the queue';
- show the same respect must to other students' families;
- be aware that I may have to inform someone else of what you have told us.

Student voice

Of course, if you are already in a school which makes full use of student voice, your students will be quite used to having their opinions canvassed. If this is the case, you will not have to work quite so hard at setting out your parameters for the discussion process. So, what exactly is student voice? Student voice describes the distinct perspectives and actions of young people on education-related matters. Student voice gives students the ability to influence learning, policies, programmes, contexts and principles. In principle, making use of student voice assumes that:

- Young people have unique perspectives on learning, teaching, and schooling.
- Their insights warrant not only the attention, but also the responses of adults.
- They should be afforded opportunities to actively shape their education.

The presence and engagement of student voice has been seen as essential to the educational process since at least the time of John Dewey who wrote extensively about the necessity of engaging student experience and perspectives in the curriculum of schools. Today, canvassing students' opinions is one way of teaching young people to have responsibility for their education. In many schools, student voice provides opportunities for young people to help choose curricula, to get involved in calendar-year planning and to make an input into school building design. Students are joining school committees of various types and at various levels. Most schools expect students to make an input into the appointment of new staff and in many schools student voice is used to shape the rules and expectations of these institutions.

So important is the notion of student voice that the English Secondary Student's Association, the representative body for secondary students in England has been created. This organization aims to support students in expressing their views about education by providing workshops and support networks with other secondary schools. The National College for School Leadership provides career-long learning and development opportunities and professional and practical support for England's existing and aspiring school leaders. Their goal is to ensure that school leaders have the skills, recognition, capacity and ambition to transform the school education system into the best in the world. I appreciate that, at this stage of your career, school leadership might appear quite a long way off. However, it doesn't hurt to start formulating your educational philosophy early on, and from a pragmatic point of view, it would do no harm whatsoever to mention your interest in student voice when attending external or internal interviews. As an experienced interviewer, I can assure you that a contribution of this type is quite rare and would really impress an interview panel.

Warning!

In light of all the advice and guidance I have given to you in this chapter, what I am now going to say to you next might now appear to be rather contradictory. In my capacity as mentor and/or assessor, I have often seen relationships get in the way of good teaching and learning. In my post-observational feedback discussions I have asked why these beginning teachers have not been more robust in their behaviour management. In the majority of cases these teachers tell me that they are reluctant to be too strict for fear of damaging their relationships with their students. These beginning teachers have totally missed the point. They have failed to note the difference between social relationships and learning relationships. You are not employed to enjoy social relationships with your students; you are in school to teach them, and your students are there to learn. Relationships with students should be cultivated in order to facilitate maximum learning opportunities and no more. If you are holding back on making decisions that would ultimately benefit learning simply because you don't want to upset your students and/or because you do not want them to think badly of you, then it is students who are running the agenda, and you are not doing your job. Next time you find yourself in a quandary about whether to change the class-seating plan or whether to admonish students for their inappropriate behaviour, do not think about *your* needs, but ask yourself what is ultimately best for them. Authoritative teachers do not court popularity but consider the needs of their students above all else. Ironically, it is their determination to follow a firm but fair policy, irrespective of what students think of them, which ultimately leads them to becoming both respected and popular.

Suggestions

- Develop and maintain good learning relationships with your students, not good social relationships
- Appoint student representatives for your tutor group
- Listen to what your students say but focus on their 'needs' rather than their 'wants'
- Hold tutor group meetings on a regular basis in order to allow a student voice
- If there is no student council in your school, then lobby for one
- Gain a student perspective on their educational diet by shadowing them in lessons
- Carry out your own research into students' perceptions of their teachers. Make sure you keep the names of the teachers in your research anonymous
- Produce your own teaching and learning survey – use the results to improve your practice
- If you have a tutor group, get your students to produce their own advert for a teacher. Use these as the basis for a discussion

4 Creating a positive learning environment for your students

A great deal of attention has been given to 'brained-based' learning over the past ten years, and quite rightly so. Anything that helps teachers to understand how students learn should be given credence. Less attention, however, has been paid to how our knowledge of the brain can help us to establish, maintain and develop good relationships with students. This chapter briefly explores the various functions of the brain. It then goes on to outline how we can use this knowledge to create a positive classroom ethos, manage our classes, and improve our relationships with students.

Dr Paul MacLean of the National Institute of Mental Health in Washington DC developed a theory that suggests that the human brain can be divided into three distinct areas. He named these as:

- the neo-cortex
- the limbic system
- the reptilian brain.

Figure 4.1 provides more detailed information.

The neo-cortex can be found at the top of the brain and functions as the cognitive, or thinking, area. It is divided into two hemispheres and joined by the 'corpus callosum'. This area of the brain is used to solve problems and to identify patterns.

The limbic system deals with our emotions, beliefs and value systems and also concerns itself with long-term memory.

However, it is the oldest evolutionary part of the brain that provides the main focus for this chapter. I believe that knowledge of the reptilian brain to

The Structure of the Brain

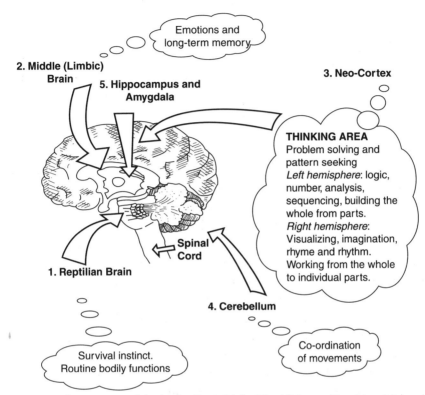

Figure 4.1: The structure of the brain. (From Dixie, *The Ultimate Teaching Manual* 2011, page 94.)

be of real relevance to the purpose of this book – that of offering advice and guidance on how to establish, maintain and develop good working relations with students.

So what do we know about the function of the reptilian brain? It is responsible for routine bodily functions such as breathing, heartbeat, blood pressure and balance. It is the primeval part of the brain that takes charge of our survival responses. The reptilian brain helps us to judge whether to stick around and fight in times of danger, or 'cut our losses' and run. Just as in the animal world, the reptilian brain predisposes us to a system of social conformity, of being able to know one's place in the pecking order of things and of possessing the need to respond to ritualiztic rules. In situations where the individual feels threatened, the reptilian brain takes over from the other two areas, and the higher order functions of the brain lose their significance. It is vital for us to have a full understanding of the role of the reptilian brain if we want to establish, maintain and develop good relationships with our students, and if we want the youngsters in our classes to learn.

Creating a physical environment that provides students with adequate light, heat, seating space and the opportunity to drink fluids will go a long way to making your students feel safe, secure, happy and ready to learn. If you do this as a matter of course, the students will be totally unaware of why they feel more comfortable in your classes. Take these conditions away, however, and you will soon notice a difference in their attitudes and behaviour. More and more schools are allowing their students to drink beverages in class, so you need to find out what the policy is in your school. I was lucky enough to have a sink in my classroom, so as long as they asked my permission, students were allowed to come up and get themselves a drink. Juice and water were allowed, but cola was banned!

But, as important as these physical prerequisites of learning are, it is the emotional conditions of the classroom that I want to focus mainly on in this chapter. In order to produce students who are happy and in a frame of mind to learn, teachers need to plan for the emotional needs of their charges. To do this they need to reduce scenarios that create anxiety, fear, lack of self-esteem, a feeling of isolation, insecurity and a sense of injustice. In short, teachers need to reduce student stress. You can do this through an understanding of the role of the hidden curriculum in your classroom. So, what exactly is meant by this term 'hidden curriculum'?

The hidden curriculum is a set of values, attitudes and knowledge frames which are embodied in the organization and processes of schooling and which are implicitly conveyed to students. Two such elements of the hidden curriculum that are relevant to this chapter are that of classroom displays and teacher–student interactions.

My advice to you, as a beginning teacher, is to take this information on board when you are planning the physical layout of your classroom. I suspect that even the most motivated and positive of teachers do not plan their classroom displays with the reptilian brain in mind. The point I want to make strongly here is that you can do a great deal to cater for the needs of your students, even before you start formally teaching them. I have provided you with a few examples from my own classroom.

One of the most important messages I wanted to get across to my students is that it is perfectly alright to get things wrong. I believe that taking risks is an integral part of the learning process, but this will not happen in a competitive learning environment. In order to establish a collaborative ethos in the classroom, I displayed a number of posters with important messages. The first of these messages is that it is 'OK to be wrong' (Dixie 2007, 2011). Displayed immediately below this poster, is a building-block model which visually demonstrated the need for my students to work together to solve problems (Figure 4.2).

When I first met my students in September, and again at key points during the year, I explained to them that each wrong answer given in lessons should be seen as a stimulus (or, a building block) for other students to take the thought process a bit further. Doing this gives even an incorrect response a degree of status! Each partially correct response acts as a building block for other students to further develop their thought patterns, and brings the class that bit closer to the desired outcome. I emphasized that the process is to be seen as *collaborative* and not individualistic. I have to say that using this approach had a dramatic effect on my relationships with my students. Students were more willing to get involved, more willing to talk to me, more willing to ask me questions and, most importantly, much more prepared to take risks in lessons. So, why exactly did this happen? Simply because they did not feel threatened! In *Managing Your Classroom* (2007), I emphasize how using this particular model can also help to dramatically reduce discipline problems in lessons.

Simply putting up posters in the classroom which encouraged students to take risks provided them with a sense of security. Explaining to the students

Figure 4.2 It's OK to be wrong! (Reproduced from Dixie, *Managing Your Classroom*, 2007, by permission of Continuum.)

that you will always be there to catch them if they fall helps to provide them with the security they need to take those risks, which are so vital to their academic and social development. I feel that the following quote from a Year Ten student really captures the flavour of what I am trying to say:

> When I arrived in the classroom, I felt insecure, but as I settled and looked around, I saw many pictures, posters and signs which help me to understand what is involved by being in the class. Students feel shy when they put their hands up, just in case they get it wrong. But in this class there are signs that say 'Take a risk' so it is much easier and less threatening when there is something telling you to take a risk and put your hand up.

It is also important for youngsters to realize that making mistakes is all part of the learning process. You need to inform them that you are doing your best to provide an environment in which they feel comfortable in showing their vulnerabilities. I displayed a couple of traditional Chinese proverbs in my classroom to get over the notion that failure is a means to success.

> He who asks a question is a fool for five minutes. But he who does not ask remains a fool forever. (Traditional)
> Failure lies not in falling down but in not getting up. (Traditional)

At the start of each academic year, I showed my students a draft copy of one of my early Master of Arts (MA) assignments. The paper was literally covered with the red biro scrawls made by my tutor. The idea behind this was to show the class that even adults have to go through this critical process during their lives. I then went on to say, however, that, providing this critical process occurs in a secure environment, they are likely to come out all the stronger for it. Hopefully, knowing this gave the youngsters in my classes some added security.

I am sure you will agree that raising the self-esteem of students has got to be a major aim of any committed teacher. However, how many of you have actually thought of making this message overt? When students entered my classroom, they were met with this message pegged up on a washing line in front of them: THIS IS A 'CAN DO' CLASSROOM. Why not pop down to the school canteen and ask if you can have eleven catering-size tins. Get these welded or wired together and display these in your classroom with the slogan 'Success comes in **cans**'.

Figure 4.3: Success comes in cans (©Peter Rennoldson, 2011).

All this seems pretty basic doesn't it? However, I assure you it works! Here is what another Year Ten student said about the culture of this classroom.

> When you walk into the room all the work on the walls shows that it is a hardworking room. The first banner on the wall – 'This is a Can Do classroom' – shows that the teacher is enthusiastic and wants us to do well. All the displays have obviously had a lot of work put into them and this tells us the teacher works hard to create a good working atmosphere. In Mr Dixie's room I want to work hard because we can tell that he works hard for us and it is only right that we do the same! The room makes me enthusiastic and gives me a positive attitude towards work.

As a committed teacher, I felt that it was important that students do their best in my lessons. You must feel the same about your classes. Again, have you thought about making your message more obvious? Setting the scene by displaying motivational posters, such as the one shown below, goes a long way to getting across to your students exactly what you expect of them.

Figure 4.4 Work with pride

Providing students with firm expectations and clear parameters can help to cater for the reptilian brain.

Never underestimate the use of primary colours and creative displays in promoting warmth and purpose in your classroom. Bright reds, complemented by an array of green plants for example, can go a long way to create a purposeful and stimulating atmosphere, and can convey to the students that they are here to work. Perhaps my most successful classroom display has been on the Great War. This particular display consisted of numerous photographs and artefacts as well as students' poetry, displayed on a background of poppy-red and white paper.

Because of the time allocated to my role as Professional Development Tutor, I didn't get the chance to teach many lower school students. However, I enjoyed inviting Year Seven and Eight students into my room when I was covering for colleagues. I liked to watch the expressions on their faces as they entered the classroom. When I heard comments such as, 'This is a brilliant classroom, sir!' or 'Cor, look at those photographs and that war helmet,' I knew that I had already got these students 'on-side'. In my all my visits to secondary schools, I can count on one hand the number of classrooms which instilled excitement and wonder in me. It is a brilliant feeling when you come across a secondary school classroom which could be mistaken for a classroom in a primary school. To provide a student perspective on this issue, I furnish you with a number of student quotes. I feel these say it all.

> When I enter the classroom first thing in the morning, I feel a sudden sense of security. Everywhere I look there is advice and information to help me through my work. The room also has a natural side to it with the plants in the corner and I like that feeling in a classroom. I prefer a classroom which makes a person feel good.

> 'When I enter this room, I feel very welcome. There are many colourful posters and motivational quotes. It makes me feel comfortable and willing to work. If the teacher has put in a great deal of effort making this room welcoming, I feel I must put in a great deal of effort into the work he sets me.

> This classroom makes me feel welcome and because a lot of effort and time have been put into it I will put effort and time into my work. It makes me motivated and gives the teacher respect as well as gives the room respect.

Students love teachers with a sense of humour. Even teenagers love jokes, no matter how bad they are. They particularly like jokes made at the expense of other members of the staff. Fortunately, I taught in a school where the camaraderie among the teaching staff was absolutely superb, and where the majority of teachers were well able to enjoy a joke at their own expense. As a result, the student–teacher relationships there were some of the best I have experienced in my career. I scattered my classroom with pages of jokes that I had adapted to suit the characteristics of some of my friends and colleagues. (Obviously, it is always advisable to seek permission before you do this.)

I accept that in the current climate of political correctness, I could be subject to some criticizm here. I also accept that, in the wrong context, using humour in such a personal way could promote a climate of vindictiveness and bullying among the students. However, you need to know that I also displayed a number of visual jokes around the classroom that were much at *my* expense. I was successful in using these to help the students to take themselves less seriously and to be able to laugh at themselves. I found therefore that, far from causing inflammatory situations, using self-deprecatory humour in this mild fashion often helped to defuse some potentially difficult situations.

When I was studying for my Masters degree, I was extremely impressed by the approach taken by my university tutors towards my learning. The tutors placed a great deal of emphasis on the holistic synthesis of mind, body and emotions, and we spent a great deal of time exploring the feelings associated with learning, as well as the subject content of the course. I recorded these feelings and emotions formally, in my learning journal. This humanist approach, inspired by the work of Maslow and Carl Rogers, was obviously an integral part of the learning programme. I like to think that I took this approach on board whenever possible in my own teaching. In my opinion, the most successful teachers don't teach subjects – they teach children. By that I mean that they are mainly concerned with the all-round development of youngsters as human beings, and not just as empty receptacles into which knowledge has to be poured. Humanist teachers place an emphasis on the personal growth of their students and on their awareness of their place in the world. The purpose of a humanist teacher is to develop a moral and social conscience in the young people within their charge. To achieve this, students need to be able to make choices and to take responsibility for their decisions. They can do this by being given opportunities to constantly evaluate their thoughts, words and actions, and by being provided with active learning scenarios. These scenarios can be offered at a conscious level through formal curriculum assignments, or at an unconscious level, through the process of student–teacher interaction and classroom display material.

With this in mind, I littered my classroom with opportunities for incidental and unconscious moral and social learning. I displayed quotes and messages on the backs of all the chairs, as well as on the walls, in the firm belief that the students would gradually subsume the meaning of these messages while they are in my room. I came into the classroom on many occasions to find youngsters discussing these quotes, some which I have included here:

Seek friends who are better than you, not your own kind. (Traditional)

Failure is the mother of success. (Traditional)

Once a word is spoken, four horses cannot drag it back. (Traditional)

Only when you know why you have hit the target can you say you have truly learned archery. (Guan Yinzi)

Any doubts I may have felt about the value of doing this were soon dispelled when I read through the following joint comments made about my classroom by two Year Ten boys.

This classroom makes us feel welcome and secure. There are many different displays and little speeches. You are bound to learn something even if it is not to do with the lesson. There are laminated quotes which don't make sense at first but, once you think about it they do make sense. They all help people in the world.

One thing I advise my beginning teachers to do is to spend five minutes or so in their classroom sitting at a desk, looking at the room from a student's perspective. Only by doing this will you be able to fully understand the potential of the classroom for unconscious and incidental learning. To further exemplify this, I asked three beginning teachers to come into my classroom, to imagine that they were students and to describe the room from a student's perspective. The results have been recorded below:

> When you enter this room, there is an immediate sense of someone who cares about the students who go in there. The room is brightly coloured and airy. There are plenty of quirky objects to look at and no end of thought-provoking mantras dotted here, there and everywhere. These really help you to believe in yourself and also provide a welcome but harmless visual distraction for those who cannot concentrate for long periods of time.
>
> My favourite part of this room is his wall display on World War 1. Every time I go in, I cannot stop looking at all the textures, photos and snippets of information that it offers. There is even a real rusty old helmet hanging from an amazing display. This is a room where positive things are expected to happen and where students are clearly encouraged to enjoy the whole process of learning. – Trainee teacher, English
>
> When I walk into Mr Dixie's classroom, I am faced with 'This is a 'Can Do' classroom' poster. I remember that it is 'OK to be wrong' here and that if I make a mistake it doesn't matter. We are here to learn and even though it's last thing on a Friday afternoon I still sit and think about what it must have been like to have been in the trenches during the war. I wonder how Mr Dixie got all that barbed wire on to the wall without hurting himself. Did they really wear those old tin hats?– NQT, English
>
> Walking into a classroom for the first time can be a daunting experience; after all you are entering new territory where you are yet to find your own space. Mr Dixie's class, in this sense, is no different. However, once you have entered the classroom you notice there is almost information overload! At first your eyes are drawn to the various posters depicting everything from pictures of the First World War trenches to posters of Ipswich Town football club, then you

realize that some of the pictures are of Mr Dixie and the students from the school. This makes you feel more at ease and relaxed. The backs of the chairs are covered with quotes and anecdotes and even jokes. All of a sudden the classroom doesn't seem as daunting as it did a few minutes ago. The layout of the desks makes it easy to move around the room, all of the resources that you need are clearly labelled and easy to find making the room 'user' friendly. The overall feel of the classroom is warm and friendly – if your mind starts to wander you find yourself reading one of the quotes or examining a picture which makes it easier to refocus your mind. A 'washing line' with posters and pictures hangs from one side of the room. It seems that wherever you look you will be drawn to bite size chunks of information and you can't help but learn something whenever you are in the room.– Graduate teacher trainee, History

A study by Kyriacou and Cheng (2009, p. 112) explored the views of over one hundred PGCE students on their attitude towards humanistic teaching in schools. A sample of student teachers was interviewed later in the year, once they had completed their first teaching practice in schools. Whereas the vast majority of the original students in the study agreed with the humanist approach, most of those interviewed after their initial teaching practice had finished, said that they found it difficult to put these qualities into practice and to maintain a positive regard for all the students in their classes. In other words, they found that the realities of classroom life had led them to temper their humanistic approach towards teaching causing them to take on a more autocratic role. My role as Professional Development Tutor in a large secondary school substantiated these findings. In some of my initial weekly seminars with my beginning teachers, many of them expressed a great deal of frustration and disappointment with the fact that their students do not seem to be responding to their humanist teaching approach. The kids are simply not being reasonable! It was beginning to dawn on them that children are not always reasonable and rational beings, and that they do not always respond positively to this rather idealistic teaching method. These teachers wanted me to tell them exactly what was missing from their lessons, and what they needed to do in order to get more disciplined and orderly behaviour from their students. I did my best to allay their concerns by telling them that, bearing in mind that they are still in the early stages of their developmental continuum, what they were feeling was quite predictable. I explained to them that their feelings were *so predictable* that I took this into consideration when designing the school's integrated ITT/NQT Professional Studies calendar.

My message to beginning teachers is not to become cynical, and not to lose sight of your early idealism or the value of using the humanist approach in the classroom. It is fair to say, however, that you may have to put some of your methods on hold until you feel that you have a classroom and behaviour management infrastructure firmly in place. When you feel you have got these students working in the way you want them to, then you can then gradually re-introduce the humanist approach. In my book *Managing Your Classroom* (2007), I place great emphasis on the importance of the establishment phase of the year, and of the need for teachers to outline their rules, routines and expectations strongly with their students. Using the humanist approach on its own, without giving due concern to the needs of students for clear and secure boundaries will simply not work. I like to feel that when I was teaching, I adopted a humanist approach with my students. However, come rain or shine, at the start of each year, and with each new class, I spent about three-quarters of an hour outlining my expectations to the students. I also spent considerable time reinforcing my behaviour regime and checking on pupils' understanding of my expectations, rules, rewards and sanctions. I would strongly suggest that you do the same. Adopt a firm and assertive manner that shows the students that you really mean business and support this approach with firm, well-considered sanctions and rewards. Something you might like to do would be to produce a Start the Year presentation pack comprising some or all of the elements outlined here: copies of your rules, routines, expectations and sanctions that students can stick into their exercise books. You are advised to support these with illustrations designed to get your message across to the visual learners in your classes. I have included an example of my expectations:

GETTING IT RIGHT!

- If the room is locked, line up *quietly* outside the room.
- Enter the room *quietly*, get your book and equipment out and work quietly on the starter tasks set for you.
- On entry to the classroom check whether you need to pick up resources from the back desk.
- Save your personal conversations with me until I am ready to talk to you.
- If you finish the set task, then stick any loose sheets into your book, remove old worksheets, underline titles and generally tidy your work up.

- At the end of the 3-2-1 countdown signal, stop talking and give me your full attention. You are to be silent when I am taking the register.

- Make sure your homework is recorded, completed and handed in on time.

- Treat the classroom with respect.

- At the end of the lesson, tuck your chairs in, pick up any litter off the floor, return your resources, stand behind your tables and wait until I give you permission to leave the room.

You are advised to constantly revisit these rules and routines as you move through the year. An effective way of doing this is to give the students a true/false quiz. I have included a few questions from one of my quizzes in Figure 4.5 below to serve as an example. Make sure that you add a 'Guess' column, informing the pupils that they can still get the points for a correct answer, but telling them that this will give you a clearer understanding of whether they understand your behaviour regime.

- A series of PowerPoint slides designed to get across to the students the notion that teaching is very much a 'deal' that requires give and take on both sides. As well as outlining what you expect from the students, make sure they understand exactly what they can *expect from you* during the course of the year. Again, I have put down a few ideas for your perusal:

  I will mark you books once a week.

  I will provide you with constructive feedback.

	RULES, ROUTINES AND EXPECTATIONS	T	F	G
1	I do not mind you being a few minutes late for my lessons		✓	
2	If the door is unlocked you are allowed to enter the room		✓	✓
3	You are expected to enter the room quietly		✓	
4	The beginning of the lesson is always a good time to have a personal conversation with me		✓	
5	You are allowed five late pieces of homework before you are put into detention	✓		✓

Figure 4.5 How well do you know my rules and routines?

I will be there to listen to you.

I will help you to celebrate your success.

- A series of motivational posters and PowerPoint slides designed to inspire, motivate and increase the self-esteem of your students. Again, I have included a few examples here.

WARM BATH – COLD SHOWER

Always celebrate success but make sure you constantly challenge youngsters and show them how to move one.

I used the following expression to explain to the students that I am there to celebrate their success but to also act as a 'critical friend':

Kites rise highest against the wind – not with it. (Winston Churchill)

These are just some of the many motivational quotes that I use in my Starting the Year presentation in September. Quotes such as these are easily obtained from the internet simply by typing 'quotations' into your search engine.

You will note that with the approach described above, there is a strong emphasis on using classroom and behaviour management strategies to set up teacher expectations in lessons. You may remember from reading Chapter One that I refer to this as a teacher's technical competence. However, you will also note that I have introduced a number of humanist elements into the presentation, such as the idea of building up good teacher–student relationships, the notion that both parties have responsibilities in the learning equation, and the importance of student self-esteem and self-expectation. I generally found that, providing I carried out the initial part of the presentation in an assertive and businesslike fashion, I was usually successful in establishing a meaningful classroom ethos for the rest of the year. However, the important thing to remember is that if you want to maintain a positive ethos in your classroom, you have to constantly remind your students of your rules, routines and expectations. Make no bones about it, failure to do so *will* result in a breakdown in relationships with your students.

Up to this point, we have discussed the merits of using a dual strategy in managing your classes for effective learning – using clearly thought-out behaviour management plans while at the same time combining this with a humanistic approach. One essential ingredient which is of the utmost importance in producing good student–teacher relationships, and good learning scenarios, relates to the degree of ownership students have of the learning process.

My experiences in interviewing students about their teachers have shown me that the most popular teachers are those who allow students to have their say and to make a positive contribution to lessons. It is fair to say, however, that in the past, most classrooms were dominated by teacher-talk, with few opportunities for students to contribute verbally to lessons. Kyriacou (2009) discusses how, even in situations where teachers did allow students to contribute verbally to lessons, these contributions were channelled along predetermined lines. The dominant message to students seemed to be that any response that did not fit closely enough with the teacher's requirements, would be rejected as being irrelevant. You will appreciate the net result of this. Students simply tapered their responses to suit the narrow remit of the question being asked. In other words, they simply had to second-guess what the teacher was thinking. I am sure you will agree that this is a far cry from the intellectual needs of students to think in a lateral and creative way. As we saw in Chapter Three, much of the reluctance to allow students to explore their own views and ideas is often down to the insecurity and low-esteem of the teacher. You, as beginning teachers, might like to consider where you stand on this issue. In an effort to gain control over proceedings in your classes, do you tend to restrict the level of verbal input into your lessons? Do you feel ready to let go yet? I have included a few suggestions that might help you to give your students greater ownership of their lessons.

Getting students more involved in class discussions and question/answer sessions

- Give your students a rationale behind your need for them to respond to your questions. Ask them to focus on the questions being asked, to formulate the necessary language required to respond, and to take a risk and put their hand up in lessons. Stress the fact that doing this is not just about being a 'boff!' As you can see from Figure 4.6, it is important to get this

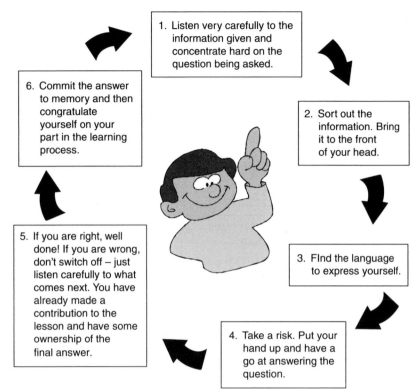

1. Listen very carefully to the information given and concentrate hard on the question being asked.

2. Sort out the information. Bring it to the front of your head.

3. FInd the language to express yourself.

4. Take a risk. Put your hand up and have a go at answering the question.

5. If you are right, well done! If you are wrong, don't switch off – just listen carefully to what comes next. You have already made a contribution to the lesson and have some ownership of the final answer.

6. Commit the answer to memory and then congratulate yourself on your part in the learning process.

Figure 4.6 Not just about being Boff

message across to your students in a visual manner. If you want to find out how I use this strategy as a classroom management tool, you need to refer to *Managing Your Classroom* 2007.

- Get your students to ask the questions. Start off the lesson by displaying some stimulus material and ask the students to come up with as many exploratory questions as possible. In other words, ask them what they want to know about the topic. I have found that giving the students greater ownership of a topic dramatically increases their participation and motivation, and most certainly strengthens the bond between myself and the class.

- There is no better way to learn about something than having to teach it to somebody else! Divide a topic area up into discrete areas and ask your students to prepare presentations. By building in a system of peer-assessment, you will be introducing a degree of status to the activity, and the students are more likely to take the activity seriously. My experiences show that the students enjoy learning in this manner. They readily admit that the additional

Rules	Rationale
You should work *together* as a group. This means you will have to plan your work *together*. Remember, a chain is only as strong as its weakest link	By doing this, you will be able to share ideas and learn from each other. You will also be able to improve your interpersonal skills
Appoint a group co-ordinator. This should be someone who is well-organized, good with people, and can motivate the group to get the work done properly	Making the right decision here rather than simply choosing your friend will help all of you in the group to succeed and to realize your potential
Find out about other people's preferred learning styles. Work to people's strengths	Doing this will allow people in the group to show what they can do and to produce a balanced presentation
Make sure you communicate effectively with other people in the group. Swap e-mail addresses, telephone numbers, and so on	Doing this means that time will not be wasted, and that you will be able to work efficiently as a group

Figure 4.7 Group-work rules

pressure of having to get things right means that they are more likely to take the material on board.

- Provide plenty of opportunities for paired and group-work activities, but make sure that your students work *together,* rather than in parallel fashion.

- Come up with a set of negotiated rules for group work. Doing this will help the students to think responsibly about the way in which they work and will, again, give them greater ownership of the lesson. If students are to gain maximum benefit from the group-work process, it is absolutely vital that you allow them the opportunity to discuss the rationale behind these rules. In Figure 4.7, I have laid out a few examples from a list of group-work rules I have negotiated with students in my classes.

- Set up a buddy mentoring system whereby students offer guidance and advice to each other.

- Accept the value of each student's contribution. Give credence and respectability to those 'lateral' thinkers in the class who come up with responses that might not be seen as 'mainstream'.

- Allow more 'wait time' (Zimpher and Howey (1987), cited in Dixie 2007) when asking questions. Giving students that extra few seconds or so to respond will dramatically increase the number of voluntary responses in class discussions and question/answer sessions.

One of the most important aspects of classroom interaction relates to the choice of words and tone of voice used by teachers in their dealings with students. Young people are extremely sensitive to the slightest critical inflexion in voice tone and/or the use of language that appears to be a personal attack on them. Many of our students are at a stage in their lives where self-esteem is low and where they may feel particularly vulnerable in front of their peers. It is imperative, therefore, that we choose our words and tone of voice very carefully. This is particularly important when we are reprimanding misbehaviour or reacting to students' responses in class discussions or question/answer sessions. As we saw in Chapter Two, difficult as this is, it is absolutely vital that, when you admonish students, you focus your attention on the inappropriate nature of their behaviour rather than on them as individuals. Do not insult students, and make it clear that there are no personal grudges behind the messages you are issuing. It is also absolutely essential that you ask the student to accompany you out of the classroom so that you do not embarrass them in front to their peers. I have included a brief example of a typical conversation I might have with a youngster who has overstepped the mark in one of my classes.

"Would you mind if I had a brief word with you outside the classroom please, Robert?" (This is said in an assertive but polite tone of voice before I turn away and walk towards the classroom door in an expectant fashion.) When we are both outside the classroom, I ask Robert to move away from the door so that we cannot be overheard by the other students inside the room. Then, in a firm but non-aggressive tone of voice, I say something like this:

> "Things are not going too well today, are they Robert – is there any particular reason for this?"
>
> Robert grunts "No, sir."
>
> "Robert, before I say anything else to you, you need to know that this is not a personal attack on you. You're a nice lad but this behaviour seems out of character to me and is not acceptable. Robert, you need to know that you are good at this subject, and that you have a lot to offer in lessons. I know you are honest enough to appreciate the fact that your behaviour is not only stopping you from learning,

but that it is also having a bad effect on the others in the class. Would you agree that this is a fair comment?

"Yes sir, sorry sir."

You will notice that in this very short dialogue, there are a lot of positive messages. First, Robert knows that it is the inappropriateness of his behaviour, and not him personally, I am criticizing. Second, by saying 'I know you are honest enough to appreciate', I am setting up positive expectations of Robert as a human being. I usually find that this low key approach is often enough to diffuse difficult situations and get the student back to work.

Always try to be positive when students give incorrect or inappropriate answers in class and try to find a way of using their responses to take the discussion further. Never put a student down for a wrong answer! If you do, they will remember it for a very long time and will be highly unlikely to volunteer a contribution again.

A great deal of sociological research has been carried out into the effect of the labelling of students by teachers. My role as a sociology teacher has heightened my awareness of this issue, and the works of Rist (1970), Keddie (1976) and Mitzos and Browne (1998) have all influenced my teaching greatly over the past fifteen years or so. So, what exactly is labelling? Basically, labelling in schools is the way in which students are encouraged and/or taught to see themselves by their teachers. As we have already seen, not all labelling is a bad thing; positive labelling can create self-belief in students and can really play a part in motivating them to succeed both academically and socially. However, we must all be very careful about labelling students in a negative way. This is often done in an overt way by referring to students as being 'nasty', 'evil', 'thick', 'troublemakers', and so on. I am not exaggerating here – my role as Professional Development Tutor required me to listen to some particularly vitriolic descriptions of students by a few beginning teachers who were struggling to get to grips with some particularly challenging classes. 'I hate taking 9M2! They simply don't want to know. They are all just a bunch of troublemakers. I'll be glad to see the back of them at the end of the year.' These teachers failed to grasp two things; first, they were taking up a defensive stance and were failing to confront their own practice; second, they were failing to see that children usually live up to the expectations placed upon them. When teachers label children, it is not surprising that these youngsters live up to these expectations. In building a positive climate we should create an atmosphere where our first assumption should be one of success, respect and high self-esteem.

Negative labelling can, of course, occur in a more subtle form than some of the examples described above show. Ignoring specific students during class discussions and question/answer sessions or using negative body language towards students can convey distaste for the student or a lack of expectations. The point I am making here is that if the students receive these negative messages enough times, they will begin to believe and internalize them. Charles Cooley, one of the early founders of the Interactionist School of Sociology, developed the concept of the 'looking-glass image' to explain the effects of labelling. The basis of his theory is that the actions of a person will very much depend upon that person's interpretation of the way they are perceived. For this reason, many interactionists place particular emphasis on the idea of 'self'. They suggest that individuals develop an image of themselves or a self-concept, and that this has an important influence on their actions. A student's self-concept depends on the reactions of others towards him/her; hence the term 'looking-glass image'. In short, we tend to act in terms of our self-image. So, if students are constantly defined as lazy, arrogant and rude, they will tend to act accordingly. You may be thinking, Surely, it cannot be as simple as that. Well, my experience tells me it is. I am suggesting to you that you take a measured look at the teaching staff in your school, that you identify the teachers who experience poor relationships with their students, and then see whether or not I am right.

Now I know that, as beginning teachers, you will be unable to do anything about what I call 'structural labelling' – that is, where the organization of the school sends out strong messages to students about their place in the institution's hierarchy. You are not in control of the way in which your school groups its students, but you are in a position to control what goes on in your classroom. You need to become aware of how much power you hold over the students by virtue of your experience and your superior use of language. In other words, you need to practise developing a positive verbal style.

There is no doubt in my mind whatsoever that, if you give considered thought to how you want the physical, social and emotional climate of your classroom to be, you can create a scenario that raises and maintains high student self-esteem. In order to achieve this you need to do a number of things:

- Make the focus and objectives for the learning transparent.
- Provide opportunities for students of all abilities to feel they have accomplished something.

- Provide opportunities for social interaction between students.
- Make encouragement and praise task-specific and not general in nature.
- Give overt and equal status to students with all types of intelligences.
- Treat your students with respect and dignity.
- Admit your mistakes to your students.

Marking with a purpose

Ask any teacher and they will tell you that the worst thing about the job is marking. It is important to realize, however, that marking students' work is not just about assessment! Whenever you take a set of exercise books home to mark, or settle down to mark a batch of test papers, think of it as an opportunity to develop, not only the learning potential of your students, but also your relationships with these youngsters. We all know that feedback to students should be formative in nature, providing them with advice and guidance about how to move on academically, setting realistic targets for them, and generally using the assessed assignment as a learning tool. However, it is important not to underestimate the power of your summative written comments as a tool for establishing and developing your relationships with your students. Using words such as 'rubbish', 'useless', and so on, will serve absolutely no purpose in either getting the youngster back on track or in helping to develop a good working relationship with that student in the future. Take as many opportunities as possible to praise your students. I always try to support my formative assessment comments with personalized comments, such as, 'You have come so far over the past year' or 'You should be really proud of your efforts here' or "Tremendous effort here.'

I would strongly advise that you not only make use of the school's credit system, but that you develop your own system for rewarding students. Quite honestly, the way I see it, the dafter the system, the better. In my classes, if students produced good work they received an Oven-Glove Award stamp, which I had made up at a local printer (Figure 4.8). The notion behind this is that their work was so 'hot' that I had to put on an oven glove to mark it! When the students obtained six of these stamps, they were then eligible for a raffle ticket which could win them a CD voucher at the end of each term. In situations where students did something exceptional, or where they made a

Figure 4.8 Feel good oven glove

consistently high effort over a long period of time, I sent one of my specially designed postcards home as a way of informing their parents.

Although, I was often referred to as 'sad' by my students, I know that they valued this recognition of their efforts more than the formal reward system. Whichever method you choose, you really must make sure you utilize some form of reward system in your lessons. Failure to do so will generally result in a lack of motivation, poor behaviour and low work rate. All of this will contribute towards a breakdown in your relationships with your students.

Strangely enough, one of the best ways of striking up good working relationships with students is through their parents. This can be done in the Parents Consultation sessions, by making personal telephone calls home, and/or through the school's reporting system. I know how many members of staff baulk at the thought of spending yet another three to four hours at Parents Consultation Evenings after a hard day's work at school. In my opinion, however, using these sessions creatively and positively can be one of the biggest potential investments you can make in a child. A successful consultation with parents can play a major part in helping to turn the youngster around in terms of their academic work and/or as far as their relationship with you is concerned. My advice to any young teacher attending Parents Evenings, would be to take the opportunity to start off the session by praising the child or by talking about the student's good qualities, even if you know that the child is being difficult or not really working up to full potential. I know what the reaction of some teachers would be to this – 'But there is nothing redeemable about Gary' or 'Quite honestly, I feel that Sharon is simply a pain in the backside. When she's not there I breathe a sigh of relief. I cannot think of anything nice to say about her.' I have actually heard teachers say that they hate some of their students. As far as I am concerned, remarks such as these say more about the teacher than they do about the students. Of course, some of these students are difficult. Of course, life would be a lot easier if they weren't your class, but the truth is that you will never get them to change their ways unless you show that you have recognized their strengths and qualities. Showing teacher warmth and a positive attitude towards their children can make a real impression on parents, and these messages are almost certainly likely to cascade directly onto the child when the parents get home.

As far as I am concerned, the same principles apply to report writing. I am extremely critical of the cut-and-paste descriptor-level style of reports used by some schools to report a child's progress today. In the past, I have been told not to 'over personalize' my reports, and instead to focus on giving information about the child's current state of learning as measured by a formal set of criteria. Of course, this is important, but unless I recognize the student as an individual, they are highly unlikely to make any progress in my lessons.

So, what happens when youngsters do not do the business in lessons? What happens if they are underachieving? Do you try to soften the blow? Do you lie? No, of course not. What you do is to make a real effort to get to know the whole child. Talk to the youngster before you write the report, get their perspective on the issue, and make it clear in your report that you like them and want to work with them to help them realize their potential. Just using such a simple phrase as: 'As much as I like Joe, it is fair to say that . . . ' At the beginning of the report get the message over to Joe that the suggestions you are going to make have been made with his best interests at heart. That's all very well when you *do actually like* the student concerned, but what on earth do you write when you really *don't* like the youngster? You must never feel guilty about not liking a student – we cannot like everybody we meet. Very often, it is really difficult to like someone who has been uncooperative, who has sworn at you or who has generally made your life hell. It is important, however, that the general tenor of your report demonstrates respect for the student concerned. In other words, you should again be focusing your attention on the inappropriate nature of the student's actions and not using condemnatory language to show your dislike for them.

Teaching, as you have probably found out, is not an exact science. You will already have received a catalogue of advice from a whole range of people throughout your short career. Some of this guidance will have been useful, while other contributions may have turned out to be inappropriate. What I have tried to do in this chapter is to furnish you with a number of approaches that have worked for me, and that have helped to develop my relationships with my students. Obviously, I believe my guiding principles to be worth considering, but how you realize these principles is down to you. Although I feel that it is absolutely imperative that you set up a positive ethos in your classroom, you must be true to yourself and you must do so in a style that is compatible with your own personality traits. If you adopt these principles, then I see no reason you should not enjoy successful relationships with the students in your classes. It is, however, very important for me to say that the setting up of a positive classroom infrastructure is not, on its own, the panacea to solving all relationship problems with your students. There will still be a number of students for whom this approach will not work and who continue to be difficult and to disrupt the learning of others. The following chapter explores ways in which you can establish and maintain good relations with these challenging youngsters, and explains how you can minimize disruption in your lessons.

Suggestions

- Get your tutor group to help you choose your colour scheme for your classroom
- Play appropriate music in your lessons
- Produce a guidance sheet on how to use specific exam skills and display this in your classroom
- Display motivational quotes and posters designed to raise the aspirations of your students
- Display posters and quotes demonstrating the qualities you are seeking to promote among the students in your classes
- Display posters and quotes that encourage appropriate 'risk taking'
- Display posters and quotes that convey the message that this is a 'Can Do' classroom
- Display interesting photographs, cartoons, sketches – just to get the students to think

- Display quiz questions and conundrums for students to think about
- Display your expectations and rules
- Use your marking to raise esteem and motivate students
- Create your own reward system – perhaps issuing raffle tickets for good work/behaviour and then having a half-termly draw

5 Understanding and supporting challenging students

It may console you to know that even good teachers have some discipline problems. Teachers who say they never experience behavioural problems in their classes are, at best, deluding themselves and, at worst, simply lying. I suspect that many of you would not expect me, as a teacher with long-standing experience, to have experienced behavioural problems with my students. This is an unrealistic expectation to hold! Of course, I did everything I could to set up an infrastructure for good discipline in my classes, but teaching isn't a static process, and students are not like robots, responding to programming. Despite the best planning, things can go wrong. There have been many occasions during my long career where, because of the actions of a few challenging students, my behaviour-management plans have been shot to pieces. In these situations, I have had to apply alternative strategies in an attempt to deal effectively with some extremely tricky situations.

Schools differ greatly in their responses to disruptive students. Some schools have on-site behavioural units, where youngsters go for a cooling off period. In some areas, however, disruptive students spend time at separate off-site units meant to keep challenging behaviour out of the classroom. There are also marked attitudinal differences in schools' approaches towards the behaviour of their disruptive students. Some schools take a sympathetic counselling approach towards this antisocial behaviour, while others are far more robust in their responses. It is not within the remit of this publication to explore the wider structural strategies for dealing with indiscipline in schools. The fundamental purpose of this chapter is to explore the agendas of disruptive students and to offer some strategies to help you deal effectively with these youngsters in your lessons.

In order for you to become successful in dealing with challenging students, you need to be fully aware of the interactive nature of teaching; a process that requires an ever-changing system of exchange and negotiation between you and your students. It is important for you to remember that it is not simply a case of you employing the 'jug and mug' principle, with the children being the empty receptacles into which you simply pour a healthy portion of knowledge. No longer should the students be considered to be the passive recipients of the teacher's subject expertize. It is important for all of us to remember that students bring their own socially constructed agendas into the classroom. These agendas have been formed through their experiences both at home and at school and manifest themselves in the idiosyncrasies, expectations, aspirations and intentions brought into your classroom. It is, therefore, to be expected that at some point during the working day, even the most effective and skilful of teachers will experience a conflict of interest between the values of the school and those of some youngsters in their classes. It is your role as a teacher to reduce the number of situations that could conflict with the ultimate aim of the lesson – that of producing an effective learning scenario for students.

So, what exactly constitutes challenging behaviour? All teachers experience some relatively minor low-level disruption in their classes from time to time. Indeed, research shows that this type of misbehaviour is far more common than more serious breaches of discipline that may occur during the year (Dixie 2007 & Wragg 1993). Usually an effective behaviour-management plan will help to eradicate these minor student indiscretions. However, the type of scenario we need to concern ourselves with in this chapter is where the behaviour of a student is such that it:

- seriously undermines the teacher's ability to establish and maintain effective learning scenarios; and/or
- threatens the safety of the teacher or that of other students in the class.

There is no doubt that this type of behaviour is on the increase in our schools today, and that it is of real concern to teachers across the country. This issue has been recognized by the National Union of Schoolmasters and the Union of Women Teachers (NAS/UWT) as being of growing concern. On their webpage they stress that, although maintaining high standards of behaviour is becoming increasingly difficult, it is important not to misrepresent the nature of the problem (NASUWT 2010).

They describe a growing weapon-carrying culture among young people, which causes concern, but then go on to say that these types of incidents in schools are still rare. They also point out that serious, widespread violence and disruption are a further concern, although they stress that such behaviour remains confined to a minority of students in a small number of schools. The main concern for staff in all schools, in all areas, is the growing pressure from what is now the most common form of poor behaviour, so-called low-level disruption. They explain that constant challenges to authority, persistent refusal to obey school rules and frequent, regular verbal abuse of staff are the hallmarks of this behaviour. They purport that if this behaviour remains unchallenged over a long period, it can have a devastating impact on the health and welfare of teachers and a dramatic loss of learning time. Hundreds of teaching hours are being lost challenging this behaviour.

I need to make it clear that I have not cited this information in order to alarm you or to initiate any kind of 'moral panic'. I am convinced that, despite these worrying trends, most student indiscipline can be eradicated through the use of good classroom management strategies and by combining a firm behaviour regime with a humanistic approach towards pupils, as described and discussed in detail in Chapter Four.

So, what exactly constitutes disruptive behaviour? If you asked teachers to describe the characteristics of students who seriously disrupt their lessons, most would easily be able to come up with a list of common inappropriate and anti-social behaviours. My NQTs and teacher trainees produced the following list during one of my behavioural management sessions:

- Making an attention-seeking entry into the classroom
- Constantly and persistently shouting out
- Making inappropriate comments
- Refusing to do any work
- Throwing things across the classroom
- Hitting or goading other students
- Being rude and aggressive
- Disobeying and challenging the authority of the teacher.

Unfortunately, these disruptive students very often display a combination of these behaviours. Unless the individual class teacher can stem the tide, a cumulative effect often tends to occur, with perhaps a minor incident finally precipitating the school's decision to exclude the student. Kyriacou (2009 classifies the most frequently precipitating incidents into five categories:

- Physical abuse, including assaults on children, teachers and other adults
- Verbal abuse, including insolence, swearing and disobedience to staff, and abusive behaviour to other students
- Disruption, including disruption in lessons, refusal to accept punishments, breaking contracts, and misbehaviour which disrupts the smooth running of the school
- Criminal behaviour, including drug-related activities, vandalizm and theft
- Truancy plus other attendance problems including absconding

It is likely that many of you will recognize these antisocial behaviours in some form or another among the students in some of your classes. It is also highly likely that many of these behaviours have underlying and interrelated causes that may not lie within the realms of the school, or within the remit of the ordinary subject teacher. Sociologists refer to these causes as 'outside school explanations for differential motivation and achievement'. These outside school explanations include such factors as parents' child-rearing practices, the physical conditions of the home environment, the stability of family relationships and the cultural attitudes of parents towards education. While it is vital that you have an understanding of the role of these factors in shaping the lives of your students, it is important for you to remember that there are limitations to what you can personally do to redress these issues in the early stages of your teaching career. It is therefore, not within the remit of this chapter to explore the argument about whether schools should or should not be expected to compensate for society. Any guidance or advice offered will be restricted to what you as subject teachers or form tutors can reasonably be expected to do in order to minimize instances of disruptive behaviour in your classes. Having said all of this, do not underestimate the importance of a friendly and enquiring word about 'how things are going at home'. As you will see later in the chapter, taking the time to talk through issues with challenging students can work wonders for your relationships with these youngsters in the classroom. However, be realistic and don't expect to be able to put these problems right entirely on your own.

We saw in Chapter Two how important it is for a teacher to be reflective. No matter how threatening the situation might seem, I would advise you to look inwardly at what you are doing in the classroom, before you resort to employing heavy-handed sanctions. 'Coming the heavy', without fully evaluating whether you have done your bit to provide a stimulating and sympathetic learning scenario, will only serve to cause hostility and resentment among your students. A study by Munn and Lloyd (2005) cited in Kyriacou (2009) that involved interviewing students labelled 'disruptive' revealed some very interesting perspectives on the issue. Many of the students interviewed felt provoked into misbehaving and talked about the teacher insulting them and being responsible for their losing their dignity and self-esteem in front of their peers. They classified these behaviours into four categories:

- Teachers who were boring
- Teachers who could not teach
- Teachers whose discipline was weak
- Teachers who made unfair comparisons.

As far as these students were concerned their disruptive behaviour was justified. They were only fighting back in a situation where they had felt under threat. It needs to be said that while these perceptions continue to exist, then quite simply, lessons will continue to be disrupted and conflict will inevitably occur. As highlighted in Chapter Three, it is important for you as beginning teachers to ascertain the perceptions of your students about the way things are going in your lessons. As we also discussed earlier, giving your students some ownership of the lessons will go a long way to reducing this conflict and help to make them feel part of the learning process.

You will probably already be aware that many behavioural problems occur in classrooms because of the increasing number of students with special educational needs. It is important to remember that a great deal of misbehaviour occurs simply because these students simply do not understand the work being set for them. These youngsters are often in a no-win situation here. If they try to do the work, they are likely to meet with frustration and failure, and then subsequently incur the wrath of the teacher. If these students opt out of doing the work, they are likely to get bored and start to distract their peers. Again, this is likely to incur the teacher's displeasure. It is vital that you, as teachers, take a step back and try to show some empathy for these youngsters. I don't know what your maths or science background is like, but mine is virtually non-existent. Whenever I start to get exasperated with students who simply cannot understand the work, I try to reproduce the following imaginary but, nevertheless, nightmare scenario.

I am sitting in a lecture hall listening to one of the world's most eminent scientists give a lecture on Einstein's theory of relativity. I am starting to panic because my tutor has asked me to take notes and to use these to make a verbal presentation to the seminar group when next we meet. I haven't got a clue as to what the professor is talking about! I look around me and notice all my friends nodding in the right places and taking reams of copious notes. My heart starts to beat faster, and I break out in a cold sweat at the thought of my task. The only way out of this situation is for me to pretend I don't care. I screw up my notepaper and fling it surreptitiously at my friend sitting to my left. He gives me a disapproving sideways look. I put my hand to my mouth, give a fake yawn, raise my eyebrows in mock boredom, and then walk out of the lecture hall in disgust thinking about all the excuses I can offer for not being able to give this feedback session.

My advice is for you to put yourself in the position of those students who find their schoolwork challenging and stressful. Try to re-create situations where you have found things difficult and where pressure to succeed has been placed unfairly upon *you*. By doing this, you will get an understanding of what many of your special education youngsters are going through. It will also help you to find the right verbal and body language to deal sympathetically with their difficulties. In addition to this, make it your business to find out about some of the more common special education needs (SEN) conditions such as attention deficit hyperactivity disorder (ADHD), autism and dyslexia. You need to use this information to cater for these students in your lessons. Although I have provided you with a brief summary of these and other conditions later in this chapter, you still need to speak to your SENCO and try to find out as much as you can about the specific needs of the individuals in your classes. You also need to be aware that when seriously disruptive students are referred to the educational psychologist, they are assessed for behavioural and emotional disorders. The former condition relates to such things as anti-social behaviour, truancy, stealing, and violence towards others, while the latter relates to such emotional behaviours as anxiety, depression, self-harm, withdrawal, problems in establishing and maintaining relationships.

If your students are displaying any of the symptoms described earlier, check your records to see if they are on the special needs register. If they have not been placed on this register, then have a word with your HOD or SENCO. These youngsters might have slipped through the net. Providing you do this, and providing that you have acted positively upon the advice offered above, as beginning teachers, you cannot be expected to do more. Having said this, I think it wise that you at least gain a rudimentary knowledge and understanding of some of the most common conditions found among students in our schools today. To this end I have produced a number of 'thumbnail' descriptions to help you to manage the needs of some the SEN students in your classes. I have chosen to explore the five conditions most likely to occur in your classrooms: ADHD, attention deficit disorder (ADD), autism, Asperger's syndrome and dyslexia.

Attention deficit hyperactive disorder

The following words taken from the ADHD Made Simple website – (www. adhd-made-simple.com/) superbly illustrate what it is like to have ADHD.

> Imagine living in a fast-moving kaleidoscope, where sounds, images, and thoughts are constantly shifting. Feeling easily bored, yet helpless to keep your mind on tasks you need to complete. Distracted by unimportant sights and sounds, your mind drives you from one thought or activity to the next. Perhaps you are so wrapped up in a collage of thoughts and images that you don't notice when someone speaks to you.

Although the condition does not manifest itself in the same way for everyone, for many people this is what it could be like to have ADHD. Students with ADHD:

- Have short attention spans, which means that they often fail to grasp the main thrust of the lesson even though they are not without academic ability
- Are usually hyperactive and find it very difficult to sit still in one place for very long
- Are quite impulsive and tend to fail to think about the consequences of their actions;
- Find it difficult to complete tasks
- Are not always fully aware of what's going on around them
- Are disorganized, often forgetting their books and/or equipment.

However, on some days and in some situations, these students can appear to function quite well, leading school staff to think the person with ADHD can actually control these behaviours. As a result, the disorder can mar the person's relationships with others, in addition to disrupting their daily lives, consuming energy, and diminishing their self-esteem.

ADHD, once called hyperkinesis or minimal brain dysfunction, is one of the most common mental disorders among children. It is interesting to note that boys are more susceptible to the condition than girls; two to three times more boys than girls are affected. ADHD often continues into adolescence and adulthood, and can cause a lifetime of frustrated dreams and emotional pain. Bearing in mind the antisocial nature of the disorder, you will not find it surprising to note that students with ADHD are often rejected by their peers and find it difficult to make friends easily. There are serious consequences to this social isolation, which can 'often lead to a lack of self-esteem, to depression and to anxiety, and can lead to the student self-harming or taking drugs. In an effort to feel wanted, many of these youngsters get in with the wrong crowd and often become involved in acts of delinquency and crime'. (Dixie 2009 p. 87)

In the last decade, scientists have learned much about the cause of the disorder and are now able to identify and treat children, adolescents, and adults who have it. A variety of medications, behaviour-changing therapies, and educational options are already available to help people with ADHD to focus their attention, build self-esteem, and function in new ways. However, there are things that you as teachers can do to minimize the negative impact that ADHD can have on the learning of the student and of the other students in the class. These actions have been listed overleaf.

Attention-deficit disorder

Attention-deficit disorder (ADD) is similar to ADHD but without the hyperactive tendency. It should be noted that ADD is more common in females than in males and is often overlooked because of the absence of the disruptive behaviour that is usually associated with ADHD. Students suffering from ADD are often extremely quiet and insular, and have a tendency to withdraw from other children. These are the students who marginalize themselves from the learning, so you need to involve them in the lesson as much as possible. As is the case with ADHD, students find it difficult to focus in lessons, and this lack of concentration tends to have a negative effect upon their academic performances. However, unlike ADHD students, who are quite robust in demonstrating their failure, ADD students often fail quietly.

So, how can you support these students?

Students with ADHD and ADD may need help in organizing. Therefore make sure that you give full consideration to the advice and guidance adapted from my book:

- Establish and maintain a particular schedule. Have the same routine for the entry phase of the lesson. Be consistent in your expectations as to lining up outside the classroom, how they should enter the room and exactly what they should do when they sit down at their desks. If you do have to change your routines for any reason, make sure that you tell your SEN students in advance and that you stay close by when they enter your classroom. Doing so will provide them with that added degree of security.

- Ensure that your classroom is highly organized and structured. Establish a place for your resources, for your teacher's desk, and wherever possible (and I recognize this may not be easy if you have a challenging class), try to ensure that the students sit in the same seats. Again, if you decide that behaviour has to improve, then talk to these students in advance and physically escort them to their new seating positions.

- Stress the importance of writing down the homework instructions, and make it your policy to check on a regular basis to see that they've done it.

- Be fair and consistent in your expectations, rules, routines, rewards and sanctions. If rules are followed, give small rewards to students. Students with ADHD often receive, and expect, criticism. Look for good behaviour, and praise it whenever you can. Use as much positive language as you can.

- When giving directions keep them short and accessible and deliver them in a measured and calm voice. If you are delivering a lesson which requires students to carry out a wide range of activities, produce an instruction checklist for your ADHD students. Include a column where they can tick off each activity when they have completed it. This will provide these students with a sense of security and give them a sense of achievement as they work through the tasks. (Dixie 2009)

Autistic spectrum disorders

Autistic Spectrum Disorders (ASDs), of which Asperger's syndrome (a high-functioning form of autism) and autism are examples, are brain-based disabilities that affect language, communication, imagination and/or information gathering. These disorders, like ADHD, mainly affect the male population. Autism is an emotional disorder characterized by a profound withdrawal from social contact, repetitive behaviour, and fear of change in the person's environment. The emotional disorder impacts upon the brain's ability to receive and process information. People who have autism find it difficult to act in a way that other people think is 'normal'. They find it difficult to talk to people and to look at people, and they often shy away from physical contact. A person who has autism tends to turn inwards. They often talk only to themselves, rock themselves backwards and forwards, and laugh at their own thoughts. They do not like any type of change and may find it very difficult to learn how to behave in new learning scenarios, such as working in groups or having to sit in a different seat. Their use of language is often pedantic, and they often have a tendency to take things literally. I remember one incident from my teaching career when I was extremely cross with one particular child's behaviour and I instructed him to leave the classroom by telling him to 'take a walk'. When I went out into the corridor to talk to him I found that was exactly what he had done. I eventually found him walking around the school grounds.

Autism appears to be genetic. Parents with an Asperger's syndrome often have children with Asperger's syndrome or more severe autism. Sometimes people who have autism are extraordinarily gifted or talented. These people are said to have savant syndrome. They are often very good at just one thing in particular, like mathematics, music or computing. About 1 to 2 of every 1,000 people have autism.

In summary, ASD students find it extremely difficult to:

- interpret the meanings behind normal everyday conversations;
- know what to say;
- have a meaningful conversation;
- make eye contact;
- volunteer verbal responses in lessons;
- form social relationships with adults and their peers;

- show empathy or concern for other people;
- behave appropriately;
- participate in group activities;
- hide their feelings;
- use their imagination;
- accept novelty or changes to their routines.

From *The Trainee Secondary Teacher's Handbook,* Dixie 2009.

If you have a student with autism or Asperger's syndrome in your class, do not panic. Students whose needs are not at the severe end of the spectrum can be and have been successfully integrated into mainstream schools. This has been most successful where schools have been given opportunities to understand the implications of Asperger's syndrome or autism for the child and have had the opportunity to explore strategies and interventions. You will need to be flexible and show recognition that the child may need some approaches different to those used for the other children. Close working with parents is also essential, to ensure consistency and mutual support.

When teaching students with autism or Asperger's syndrome in a mainstream school you will need to take into account the following issues:

- The student's inability to generalize learning (every situation appears different to the student)
- The lack of incidental learning (everything needs to be directly taught)
- The literalness of understanding
- The student's difficulty understanding abstract concepts
- Difficulties in becoming involved in group activities including play and games
- Possible reactions to over-stimulation and the fact that this can easily occur in situations that other children cope well with
- Observed disruptive behaviours and non-compliance may in fact have a range of other meanings for the child with autism or Asperger's syndrome (i.e. the perceived disruptive behaviour may in fact be the student's way of

indicating the need for help or attention, or to escape from stressful situations, of obtaining desired objects, of demonstrating his/her lack of understanding, of protesting against unwanted events, of gaining stimulation).

So, what can you do to support these students with autism?

Some basic strategies you could use to effectively manage the relationships and the learning of the students with autism in your classes could include:

- Provide them with a very clear structure and a set daily routine. If you are a form tutor, you could ensure that the student knows the day's programme at the start of each day. You can do this by going through their timetable and helping them to get mentally and physically prepared for each lesson.

- Warn them students of any impending change of routine or switch of activity.

- Use clear and unambiguous language. Avoid humour/irony, or phrases like 'my feet are killing me' or 'I'm laughing my head off', which will cause bewilderment.

- Provide students with visual examples of abstract concepts. The following words from Temple Grandin an author with autism and cited in Paxton and Estay (2007) make this point extremely well:

Growing up, I learned to convert abstract ideas into pictures as a way to understand them....The Lord's Prayer was incomprehensible until I broke it down into visual images. The power and the glory were represented by a semicircular rainbow and an electrical tower.

- Use an individual's name when addressing the class. Students with autism often do not realize that the general instructions given to the class are also meant for them.

- Repeat instructions and check understanding. You need to speak in a measured and clear manner, using short sentences to ensure clarity of instructions.

- Use a variety of presentation styles – visual, physical guidance, peer modelling, and so on.

- Recognize that some change in a student's manner or behaviour may reflect anxiety (which may be triggered by a [minor] change to routine).

- Not taking rude or aggressive behaviour personally and recognizing that the target of the student's anger may be unrelated to the source of that anger.

- Teach specific social rules/skills, such as turn-taking, learning to lose and the concept of social distance.

- Minimizing/the number of distractions for your students. Some students find colourful and stimulating classrooms difficult to deal with, while others cannot cope even with general background noise. See if you can provide a booth for your students to work in.

- Link the work covered in lessons or set for homework to the student's particular interests.

- Use word-processing, and computer-based learning to help support students' literacy.

- Protect the student from teasing during breaks and lunchtime, and provide peers with some awareness of his/her particular needs.

- Allow the student to avoid certain activities (such as sports and games) which she or he may not understand or like and which cause them some distress.

- Support students when they are involved in group tasks.

Dyslexia

Dyslexia is a complex learning disability that mainly affects spelling and reading, although the disorder can also cause students to experience difficulties with writing and number work. Many people go through their lives without having their dyslexia diagnosed, but they manage to devise their own coping strategies to get by. In the past these students would have been labelled as being thick, stupid, backward or lazy. As teachers it is important for us to remember that dyslexia is not linked to intelligence. I remember one particular lad in my geography class who received support from a Learning Support Assistant (LSA) for the two years of his Geography General Certificate of Secondary Education (GCSE) course, and then went on to gain an 'A' grade in his examination. It is up to us to us to remember to teach inclusively if we want these students to succeed. To do this we need to be able to recognize the characteristic behaviours of students who have dyslexia. To this end, I have provided a list of common symptoms overleaf:

- *Sequencing:* Students who have dyslexia get very confused with the sequences of numbers or letters that make up a date or spell a word.

- *Speech:* Students with dyslexia are often able to demonstrate good verbal ability, but this is not matched by their use of the written word. Poor spelling is often a big issue with these students.

- *Late development:* Many youngsters with dyslexia are slow to learn speech, tell the time, and many get confused between right and left. They may also experience difficulties with their motor skills such as catching, throwing, skipping and jumping, all of which require some degree of sequential thought. This is particularly relevant for the Physical Education (P.E.) teachers among you.

- *Reading:* Students with dyslexia really struggle with reading, often complaining of letters being jumbled up. They often get their letters mixed up when reading text, for example, mistaking *b*'s for *d*'s and vice versa. Students with dyslexia will often do everything they can to avoid reading in class, especially out loud.

- *Concentration and memory:* Students with dyslexia often have difficulty concentrating for long periods of time. It is also true that their short-term memory may be poorer than their peers. As a result of this, they may be very slow to complete the tasks you set them in class and may not be able to finish them.

- *Achievement:* In most cases, students with dyslexia underachieve.

If you want to establish and maintain good learning relationships with these students you need to know how to get the best out of them: With this in mind, I have provided you with guidance on how to do this below.

So, how can you support students with dyslexia?

- Make sure that these students are clear about the main points of the lesson before you start teaching it. Constantly check their understanding of what you have told them. Provide a verbal summary of what you have taught them before. Having done this, ask them what they have understood and not understood. Make sure that you praise, reinforce and correct where necessary.

- Do not refer to them as 'dyslexics'. Using this term creates a master label for a student that does not do justice to the qualities and characteristics of the whole person.

- Provide regular breaks, especially if the activities require them to concentrate for long periods of time.

- Integrate them with the rest of the class wherever possible.

- Take full account of their condition when marking their work, and do everything you can to promote a positive attitude towards their learning and self-image.

- Use mind maps with these students when you can.

- Make sure that you constantly repeat your instructions, but do so in a patient manner.

- Adopt a positive attitude towards dyslexia. Avoid using such terms as 'overcoming', 'disability', 'handicap' or 'drawback'.

- Always write down the homework and other instructions, which you might expect other students in the class to remember.

- Provide them with scaffolding when helping them to organize their work.

- Never ask them to read out loud, or ask them to read a form or to sign something on the spot.

- Always liaise with the SENCO about these students.

When you interact with your SEN students, it is important to remember that 'a frustrated child is an unhappy child'. This frustration can often manifest itself in a display of disruptive and antisocial behaviour. It is worth you doing everything you can to eradicate, or at least reduce, the causes of their frustration. This can be achieved by using the advice and guidance proffered above when planning your lessons.

Pre-empting challenging behaviour

So you have implemented all the advice and guidance about setting up a positive classroom ethos, as described in Chapter Four, but there are still a number of students whose behaviour you are finding difficult to deal with. What do you do?

As with your behaviour/classroom management plan, there are a number of things you can do to prevent conflict and to avoid your lessons being seriously disrupted by these challenging youngsters.

- Get to know what makes these students tick. Read all their records, talk to them, to their form tutors, to their Heads of Year and, if you feel able to, find out from their parents what they are like at home. By doing this, you will be able to get a 'feeling' for the students concerned.

- Go out of your way to be friendly to these youngsters when you see them around the school, even if you have had trouble with them. Ask them how they are. Ask them what they did over the weekend. As I stressed in *Managing Your Classroom* (2007), often the mere act of using a student's name and talking to them as real people, is akin to making psychological contracts with them. Even if they are looking for trouble, students find it more difficult to misbehave when, perhaps in the corridor half an hour earlier, you were asking them how their football match over the weekend went.

- Find a slot to talk formally with these individual students. Notice that I said talk *with* and not *to*. Often, challenging and disruptive students have study periods allocated to them when they have been excluded from some of their classes. If your non-contact periods coincide with any of these, use this time to find out about these students. I can almost hear you say, I am too busy to do this. My response to you is simple – if you don't make the effort, you will end up more stressed, and you will spend far more time sorting out discipline problems than had you adopted a more proactive position in the first place.

- Get involved in extra-curricular activities, such as sport, drama, school clubs, and school trips. Find common interests with your students. Some of the biggest rogues in my school belong to the school football team. Football is a particular passion of mine and often is the focus of much discussion between these students and myself. Take time to notice and comment upon qualities displayed by your challenging students in these activities. 'You're a really good team player, Nathan!', 'You showed real strength of character today, Gary'!, 'You've got your team really playing well for each other Shelly'! or 'You're a born leader Michael!'

- Observe the body language and facial expressions of these youngsters before they enter the classroom. This can really help to inform the way you interact with them in your lessons. Just making a reflective statement about the way the student looks conveys care and concern to them and can act as a calming effect on the situation. You could say something like: 'You don't look very happy today, Aaron. Things not going well? Hang on here a minute, I'll get the rest of the class in and settled and we can have a brief chat.' Although, you are often not in a position to sort the problem out for the youngster, just showing that you care enough to ask how they are feeling is sometimes enough to get him or her to behave in your class, simply out of loyalty to you. If any issues crop up that you do not feel confident in dealing with, tell the student that you will do your best to find someone who can help them.

- Create a private way of communicating. Something that worked for me is to establish a private signal between the student and myself. For example, the student can make a letter 'T' (for 'time out') with their fingers to signify that he or she need a brief cooling off period outside the classroom. The knowledge that they have an 'escape clause' during the lesson acts as a form of security and is often enough to keep them in the classroom and on track.

- Don't let the student wander in the corridor. If the youngster needs to leave the room, arrange for them to go somewhere safe where they feel secure. Perhaps a colleague could supervise them in an office or an empty classroom. However, it is absolutely vital that your colleague is supportive of your methods, and does not immediately start to launch into the student about the inappropriateness of their behaviour.

- Tell the student that you need their help. You could, for example, ask them to help another youngster in the room with their work. Doing this gives off two messages; first, that you trust them, and secondly, that they have something to offer and are useful. Remember that it is vital to raise the self-esteem of these youngsters.

- Know your students well. This enables you to provide appropriate materials and topics that interest them. You can ask some of your more challenging students to launch the lesson by talking about specific issues they know about, or by bringing in items or artefacts relating to the topics under study. Again, being the 'expert' can often do wonders for student self-esteem',

- Choose these youngsters for leadership roles. This often works to raise their self-esteem. You could, for example, make them captains of class quiz teams.

- Go with the flow. Do not try to do battle on behalf of the conformist middle classes. Do not be too judgemental, and try to accept that you will never be able to totally stop these youngsters from doing what is considered by most people to be socially unacceptable. Be realistic, and accept that you will not be able to alter what has taken them over a decade to learn outside school. Just focus your attention on small-scale improvements in their behaviour and continue to make the point that the negative behaviour being exhibited is unacceptable in your lessons.

- Don't let yourself be intimidated by the physical size of student. It is important to remember, that even the biggest and most truculent youths, are frequently insecure and vulnerable on the inside. Do not, therefore, under any circumstance, use sarcasm to belittle the student or as a means of gaining control of a situation.

- Do not beat yourself up if all of these methods fail. At this stage of your career you will not have been able to build up a reputation among the school population for fair play and honesty. This takes time and is bound to include a number of failures on the way. Just let the students know you care, and refer the issue to a senior and respected colleague.

In addition to these relationship aspects, it is wise to adopt a structured and measured approach towards your teaching. Table 5.1, from the Qualifications and Curriculum and Assessment Authority for Wales (QCAAW), provides an excellent guide which will help you to anticipate and pre-empt potential behavioural issues and, as a result of this, will help you to enjoy fruitful and positive relationships with your students.

Understanding the needs of the adolescent

I am confident that in applying the strategies outlined in this chapter that you will be successful in establishing and maintaining good learning relationships with the majority of your students. However, no system is foolproof, and it is fair so say that you may need to do substantially more work with your classes. There is a point when you are going to have to go beyond being pragmatic and will need to try to get under the skin of your challenging students in order to try to fully understand them. With

Table 5.1. Checklist for promoting learning behaviours

Classroom Organization	Classroom Management	Rewards/ punishment
All equipment accessible	Arrive on time	Relate to learning behaviour
Ambient temperature	Clear instructions	Fair and consistent
Lighting/ventilation	Acknowledge positive behaviour	Achievable and relevant
Materials labelled	Acknowledge achievement	Understood by all students
Facilitate easy movement	Act as a role model	Understood by parents/carers
Positive student grouping	Differentiated learning	Respond incrementally to students' actions
Working environment purposeful, orderly, friendly and supportive	Varied pedagogy	
Work displayed	Use learning support (teaching assistants)	
Student involvement in class layout	Use peer-support	
Routine for distribution of materials	Emphasize students' roles	
	Sets of rules and routines	
	Negotiated rules/routines	
	Displayed rules/routines	
	Reinforce rules/routines	

Source: Adapted from *Challenging Pupils: Enabling Access*, QCAAW, 2000. © Crown copyright Welsh Assembly Government.

most students, having an understanding of what it's like to be young, is usually enough to get you through the day. However, I do feel that in extreme cases the need to understand adolescent behaviour is heightened. So, what exactly is adolescence and what constitutes typical adolescent behaviour?

Adolescence is a complex stage of human development occurring roughly between the ages of 12 and 18 which results in a number of major life changes for the youngster. During these teenage years the young person experiences puberty, which often has a dramatic impact on their physical, physiological and psychological systems. As if they haven't got enough to deal with, teenagers also experience a significant maturation of their cognitive functions. Both of these dramatic changes impact upon the self-image and self-esteem of teenagers, and these in turn affect their ability to establish and maintain relationships with their peers and with other adults. You will appreciate that in a school setting these changes hold particular relevance for you when you are planning your groupings and learning activities.

I am full agreement with Coleman (Moon and Mayes 2005), who see adolescence as a transition between childhood and adulthood and who stress that this transition is facilitated by a number of pressures being exerted on the young person. Some of these pressures are internal (physiological and emotional) while others, such as peer pressure, parental and teacher pressure, and pressure from society at large, are external.

Teenagers react to these pressures in different ways and to varying degrees, and as a result, move towards adulthood at differing rates. Whatever the speed of change, you will appreciate that for many teenagers adolescence is a confusing period of their lives. It is a time when they receive mixed messages from a wide range of people and where many of them are left feeling in 'no man's land'. To me, this quote from an unknown source sums up this feeling quite appropriately: 'Adolescence is where evolution says you're a grown-up but where a grown-up says you're a child.'

Changes bought about by puberty

You might be tempted to think that matters relating to puberty are unrelated to your job as teachers and that these issues can and should be left at home. Well, you would be wrong in thinking this. Puberty has a range of physiological effects which are not always outwardly apparent to observers, but which can nevertheless have a dramatic effect on the individual concerned. In addition to this, rates of maturation very enormously, making it difficult to establish and justify what a 'normal' young person is, or should be, at any given age. Early or late developers, for example, face particular problems when interacting with their peers in learning scenarios such as Drama, Dance and PE where image and self-esteem play a major part in motivation and the learning process.

In addition to the changes in the reproductive system and sexual characteristics, puberty brings about other important changes in teenagers. One of the many physical changes associated with puberty is the growth spurt – the accelerated rate of increase in height and weight that occurs during early adolescence. This in itself is a major cause of concern to many young people who often fail to fully understand what is happening to their bodies. Because growth spurts occur in different people at different times, it is not surprising that many young people are so worried about being different from their peers.

Sexual maturation is closely linked with these physical changes, the sequence of events being eighteen to twenty-four months later for boys than for girls. Again, individuals mature at very different rates; one girl at the age of 14 may be small, have no bust and look like she did in childhood, while another girl of the same age may be mistaken for a fully developed adult woman. You will appreciate the psychological effect of this on youngsters in both of these scenarios.

Changes brought about by a maturation of cognitive ability

Changes in intellectual functioning during the teenage years have major implications for you as teachers. These changes often bring with them a youngster's need to strive for independence in both thought and action. For the first time in their lives, many youngsters contemplate a life in the future when they might be able to enjoy successful relationships and make a useful contribution to society. For us as teachers, it is important that our students have some notion of the future as it helps us to motivate them and makes it easier to justify the rationale for many of our learning scenarios.

No discussion of the changes in cognitive ability can take place without mentioning the seminal works of Jean Piaget, the Swiss psychologist who first pointed out that a qualitative change in the nature of mental ability, rather than just an increase in cognitive skill, is to be expected at or around puberty. The formal operational stage begins at approximately age twelve and lasts into adulthood. During this time, people develop the ability to think about abstract concepts. Skills such as logical thought, deductive reasoning, and systematic planning also emerge during this stage.

Logic:

Piaget believed that deductive logic becomes important during the formal operational stage. Deductive logic requires the ability to use a general principle to determine a specific outcome. This type of thinking involves hypothetical situations and is often required in science and mathematics.

Abstract Thought:

While children tend to think very concretely and specifically in earlier stages, the ability to think about abstract concepts emerges during the formal operational stage. Instead of relying solely on previous experiences, children begin to consider possible outcomes and consequences of actions. This type of thinking is important in long-term planning.

Problem Solving:

In earlier stages, children use trial-and-error to solve problems. During the formal operational stage, the ability to systematically solve a problem in a logical and methodical way emerges. Children at the formal operational stage of cognitive development are often able to quickly adopt an organized approach to solving a problem.

In addition to this, Piaget's research set the ball rolling for subsequent psychologists to explore children's moral development. Coleman in Moon and Shelton Mayes (2005) explains that Piaget and Kohlberg saw two major stages of moral thinking. The first of these he called 'moral realism', which sees children making judgements quite dispassionately and on an objective basis. At this stage children's thinking is rigid and the world tends to be 'black or white'. Rules are important and must always be obeyed. For example, it is always important to tell the truth ('you smell!') even if it hurts someone's feelings. Consequences are more important than intentions – for example, even accidental/unintentional damage should be punished. Naughty behaviour should always be punished, and there is no concept as yet of making amends. Piaget describes the second stage as 'moral relativism' which sees children becoming more flexible in their moral thinking. Although they begin to understand different perspectives of right and wrong, they also understand the idea of a white lie. They understand the need to consider intentions as well as actions. Kohlberg (1969) explored Piaget's idea further. Using a series of hypothetical dilemmas presented to young people of different ages, he felt able to classify six stages of children's moral development and was able to purport from this research that an almost identical sequence appears to occur in widely different cultures. Although this is not the place for us to explore Piaget's or Kohlberg's theories in any real depth, you do need to understand the consequences of their research on your practice as a teacher.

Children reach the stage of moral relativism at different ages. You can have students who arrive at secondary school being quite able to cope with complex moral dilemmas. Equally, you may have students nearing the end of their secondary school careers who still have a rather simplistic view of the world. It is up to you to introduce moral questions into your teaching and to provide students with opportunities to discuss a range of moral issues and dilemmas.

The degree to which individual students are able to make moral decisions will also impact upon your ability to engender harmonious relationships in your tutor group and subject classes. It will affect the amount of bullying, gossiping and backbiting that goes on in your classes and will ultimately have an effect upon the amount of learning that goes on in your lessons.

Changes brought about in social relationships with adults

As we have already identified, one of the central themes of adolescent development is the young person's strive for independence. You've just got to read the words of the 'She's Leaving Home' track on the Beatles' *Sergeant Pepper's Lonely Hearts Club Band* album to see the effect of this behaviour on the adults left behind. Having said this, it is fair to say that for most young people today, this desire for independence is not demonstrated by such a grand gesture as that displayed in this Beatles' song. Independence is much more likely to mean young people having the freedom to make new relationships and having far more, say, in decisions about their education, vocation, politics and beliefs. Sociologists see adolescence as the start of a redefinition of young people's roles and status, and of their social mobility within a hierarchical social structure which is dominated by adults. I have used the word 'start' in my previous sentence because the young person's transition to adulthood is far from straightforward. While independence is usually the ultimate rewarding goal, the teenager will often 'wobble' at the thought of the frightening prospect of eventually having to become an adult. On those occasions you are likely to find your students resorting to the safety of childhood, where they are reluctant to take responsibility for their actions or future development. As teachers, you need to recognize this, and do all you can to reassure your students and coax them out of their emotional hiding places. I can assure you that dealing effectively with students who display contradictory behaviours and whose actions waiver between those of a responsible adult and those of a primary school student, is not easy. Having said this, you also need to be aware that we as adults give our students mixed messages. On the one hand, we want to them to behave in a responsible and responsive manner and to adopt an enquiring approach to learning, but on the other, we sometimes get defensive when they use their increasing critical abilities to question the type of work we give them. It is also fair to say that the green-eyed monster of jealousy can rear its ugly head, with some adults exhibiting this in response to the opportunities and idealism of youth. However, if you have read this much of the book, this is highly likely that you are the type of person who will enjoy the company of young people, rather than feel jealous of them.

Although I am no psychologist, I feel that my experience and my background reading allow me to offer a list of features generally associated with adolescence. These are:

- moodiness and mood swings
- argumentativeness
- a tendency to challenge authority
- hypersensitivity to criticism
- a sense of isolation and persecution
- unnecessary risk taking
- confused identity
- being hyper-critical of others
- fluctuating self-esteem
- difficulties in making sense of the world and establishing own values and beliefs
- preoccupation with image

- obsession with sex and relationships
- conflicting needs that waiver between wanting to be independent and wanting to belong.

The following observation made by Louise Kaplan, the twentieth-century psychologist (1984) sums up the uncertain world in which the adolescence lives: 'Adolescence represents an inner emotional upheaval, a struggle between eternal human wish to cling on to the past and the equally powerful wish to get on with the future.'

Let's face it, this degree of emotional upheaval and stress is hard enough to bear for the most stable of people, let alone for youngsters who may come from emotionally and physically disadvantaged backgrounds.

Effective relationships with all students, but particularly with challenging individuals, must come from our knowledge of what the needs of human beings are. A teacher, therefore, needs to know about 'the human givens'. So, what exactly are these?

Human givens are what we are born with. They are our genetic endowment – our physical and emotional needs that have been programmed into us throughout the course of history. Human givens also include the resources that nature has provided us with to help us get those needs met.

Those teachers who show an empathic understanding for the human givens of young people, are more likely to establish and maintain good working relationships with their students. Whether you possess a formal understanding of these needs, or whether you do this intuitively, is irrelevant. What is important is that you actually demonstrate your understanding of the needs of your students and that you do everything you can to furnish them with the resources to meet these needs. Take a look at the following lists of emotional needs and resources and ask yourself what you do both in and out of the classroom to support your students.

Emotional needs

- security – stable family life, safe living environment
- being able to make autonomous decisions
- having a sense of belonging in the community
- the need to be noticed and to receive attention

- the need for human attachment through friendship, love and intimacy and emotional attachment to others
- the need for status and self-esteem
- the need to understand the world they live in.

Resources

- long-term memory
- curiosity and imagination – to help solve problems
- the ability to understand the world and other people through story and metaphor
- the ability to be reflective, objective and self-aware
- the ability to empathize with others
- a rational objective mind that can 'side-skip' emotions and solve problems
- an imagination that can show a different world.

As teachers, we need to know a number of things; first, that many young people have problems because their physical and emotional needs are not being met in their lives. Whereas it is not possible for you, as beginning teachers, to compensate for the deficient home background of these young-sters, there are things that you can do to help your students build up a set of resources that will help them to cope with challenging situations. Here are some suggestions:

- Provide opportunities for rational thinking and for solving social problems in your classes. You could, for example, set up problem-solving group work that explores specific social dilemmas. These could relate to such issues as divorce, relationships and poverty.
- Use fiction and non-fiction materials to demonstrate alternative ways of seeing. the world, and as a means of encouraging empathy for the lives of others.
- Encourage discussion groups to explore current social issues.
- Encourage the use of a reflective journal by students.
- Encourage the need for students to take responsibility for their own actions.

We should also be aware that the mind and body are inextricably inter-twined and that the emotional brain, when highly aroused, is likely to inhibit thought and objectivity. Hopefully, you will now begin to see the need to calm youngsters down before they start to behave inappropriately and do something they might later regret.

Producing behaviour-management plans

In Chapters Two and Four, I described the importance of establishing a class-room infrastructure conducive to producing good discipline and successful learning. I have also written at length about the necessity for teachers to use the appropriate language of correction when dealing with the disruptive behaviour of classes or individuals. In this chapter, I have taken things a stage further and have attempted to focus your attention on children whose behaviour and attitudes seem to be beyond this level of planning. We have explored reasons why some of these children become difficult at school, and I have suggested a number of general strategies you might use in order to improve your working relationships with these youngsters. What happens, however, when you feel you have tried all of these and yet nothing seems to have worked?

Picture this scenario. You have got a couple of students in your lesson who are, yet again, being particularly difficult. With ever increasing volume, you hear yourself saying the same things over and over: 'How many times have I told you . . . '; 'Do I have to keep telling you . . . '; 'Will you please stop . . . ' The question that needs to be asked is whether you feel these tactics have been successful in helping you to modify the behaviour of these youngsters. It is highly likely that these strategies are not working. So, where do you go from here? This is where a behaviour plan comes in. A behaviour plan consists of an agreed strategy between the teacher and the individual whose behaviour needs modifying. There are different types of behaviour plans. Some can be formal written documents that involve parents and other staff, while others can take the form of a personal verbal contract between teacher and student. The notion behind a behaviour plan is that the teacher and student negotiate short-term and/or long-term targets for the student, to help him/her to real-ize these goals. It is important to remember that it is this negotiation process that is *so* vital to the success of the plan. If things have got particularly bad, you may have got to the point where your relationship with a specific student has all but broken down. If this is the case, you will need to bring in a third party, perhaps the student's form tutor, to broker the deal. See this process as a strength and not as a weakness!

The rationale behind behaviour plan is the fundamental belief that children can be helped to:

- recognize and understand the reasons for their behaviours
- improve their problem-solving skills
- explore choices in their behavioural responses
- explore and accept the consequences of their actions.

In the initial phases of designing your behaviour plan, it is important that you adopt a realistic attitude about what can be achieved, and that you are not too ambitious. Bearing in mind that many of these youngsters already see themselves as failures, it is vital to build a high degree of success into the early part of the plan. What I have done below is to offer you a suggested route through a behaviour plan from inception right through to its logical conclusion. However, there are two major caveats for you to be aware of. First, I have described the process in its absolute entirety; you may prefer to take a more informal approach that does not involve so many other formal contributions to the process. Secondly, know that simply because this system has worked for me, it will not necessarily be appropriate for you. Read though my suggested strategies; take from them what you will, and take full ownership of any system that you find works.

Stage 1: Identifying inappropriate behaviour

If you have read and inwardly digested the contents of this chapter it should be relatively easy to identify those students for whom the implementation of a behaviour plan is appropriate. The types of youngsters you need to target are those for whom your classroom-management plan has not worked, and all your attempts to strike up a good working relationship have failed. As a teacher, I carried out a number of surveys among my NQTs and teacher trainees; they consistently came up with the following list of persistently annoying behaviours from some of their students. These are as follows:

- shouting out answers in class
- making inappropriate and lewd comments
- swearing
- taunting or fighting with other students
- constantly getting out of their seats and wandering around the classroom
- being late for lessons and then making an entrance
- talking to other students when the teacher is talking

I am sure you will agree that these types of behaviour can have a negative effect on your relationships with the other students in the class and can ultimately erode your self-confidence and ability to teach well.

Stage 2: Setting up the process.

As beginning teachers you need to be particularly careful about treading on other people's toes so you must, therefore, try to be sensitive to the work carried out by other members of your school team when you are preparing to put your plan into action. There are a number of people you need to consult before you set about implementing your behaviour plan. In Figure 5.1, I have laid out some of the questions that need to be addressed before you make arrangements to meet the student concerned.

Stage 3: Meeting with the student

There are a number of reasons why it is important to hold a formal meeting between you and the youngster for whom the behaviour-management plan is going to be put into operation. I have laid these out below:

- **Building a rapport**. If your behaviour plan is going to stand any chance of working, it is vital that you use the meeting to build up a rapport between the two of you. You will only be able to do this if the student feels comfortable in your presence. Find a quiet private space and allocate plenty of time to the process. Try to make the youngster feel special. Provide them with a drink (and, if you are feeling generous, a few biscuits). Pay particular attention to establishing and maintaining a relaxed body posture and use a friendly and

With whom do I need to consult?	Discussion questions
Head of Department	Does the behaviour of this student warrant a behaviour plan? Is your proposed strategy appropriate for this specific student? Have you used the assertive discipline policy consistently? Have you used the departmental sanctions to support your classroom discipline plan? Is this a battle you can win? Is the return likely to justify your investment?
Head of Year Form Tutor	*All of the questions shown above.* Plus: Are there any relevant home background issues you should know about? Is there a pattern to the student's poor behaviour? Time of day/ types of lesson; time of the week? Have you consulted your Head of Department? Have you kept Head of Year and Form Tutor informed of the issues?
SEN co-ordinator	Have you read the SEN files? Are you aware as to whether the student has got a 'condition' and whether medication is being administered? If so, are you clear about the characteristics of this condition? Are you aware of the implications of this condition on the student's behaviour and learning?
Parents	Why have you contacted them? What can they do to aid the process? Do you want to know what the child is like at home? How can they reward successful outcomes?

Figure 5.1 Behaviour plan checklist

supportive tone of voice. Make sure that you outline the issues and session objectives to the student: ensure sure that you stress that the session is all about looking for a way forward, and not simply about you taking an opportunity to criticize their behaviour. Ensure that the student knows that you are not there to personalize the issue! It is also very important to listen carefully to what the youngster is saying and how they are feeling. Make it clear to the youngster that you are listening. You can do this by repeating what they say and reframing their responses. You could say something like 'If I am hearing you correctly, what you are saying is . . . ' or, 'Let's see if I've got this right. The way you see the situation is . . . ' or, 'It is important to know how you feel in this situation. Judging by what you are telling me, you feel . . . '.

- **Information gathering:** One of the main reasons for the meeting is for you to find out exactly what is causing this student to behave inappropriately. Wherever possible, therefore, make your questions open-ended so that you can then afford the student an opportunity to explore the reasons they are behaving in this particular manner. Asking closed questions will restrict the students to talking about those issues that *you* have mapped out to be the cause of their disruptive behaviour. Remember that it is just as important to explore the emotions of the students as it is to establish the facts of the case. We discussed earlier in the chapter how students bring their own socially constructed agendas into the classroom with them. If you are having problems with particular students then it could simply because their perspective about the way they are being treated is different to yours. It is very important therefore, to take time to elicit the beliefs and perceptions of the students. In order for youngsters to be able to modify their behaviour, they have to know exactly what it is they are doing that needs changing, why they are behaving in this manner and how things might look to other people. This process is called **mirroring**. The initial part of the discussion should, therefore, focus on the reasons behind the student's anti-social behaviour. As we have already explored, very often the situation revolves around the issues of self-esteem and power. Your choice of language at this stage of the proceedings is vital. You will get absolutely nowhere if you simply start to read off a list of the student's faults. You need to involve the student as much as possible in the process and get them to explore their own behaviour and the reasons behind their actions. As soon as you tell the student that you *know* the reasons for their misbehaviour, you have had it! Make sure, therefore, that at this point you ask or suggest but not tell, using phrases such as:

- To me, bursting into the room once the lesson has started shows that you might be seeking my attention? What do think about this?

- You seem to be the type of person who needs to have some control over what you do. (That is not necessarily a bad thing.) Do you think that this could be one of the reasons why you don't like being told what to do'?

- I've got a suggestion to make about why you might be getting yourself into a bit of bother – let me share this with you and you can tell me what you think.

Very often, the youngster is not fully aware of what their actions look like to other people and you should try to use this opportunity to demonstrate or mirror their behaviour. First, it is very important that you ask the permission of the student to do this and, secondly, that you don't ridicule the youngster in any way.

Tempting as it is, you need to hold off giving advice at this stage. You need to explain that the process involves the two of you working together towards gaining an agreed set of actions that will help to alleviate some of the anti-social behaviours exhibited by this student. However, it is imperative that the youngster comes to his or her own conclusions about the possible ways forward.

- **Setting goals and agreeing strategies:** One of the main purposes of your dialogue with the student is to bring about a change in their behaviour. In order to do this, targets need to be set and goals need to be realized. It is very important to make these goals achievable but, if you feel that this is not going to be possible to do all in one go, you need to break the goal down into manageable, achievable and realistic sub-goals. For example, if you know that your student would find it difficult not to call out in class for an entire lesson, then break up the lesson into, say, ten-minute time slots, and ask the student to keep a record of the number of complete time blocks they manage to control themselves. Let's take another example: A student in one of your classes cannot seem to stop swearing. You know that no amount of nagging is really going to alter his behaviour. What do you do? Although I feel that extrinsic rewards are important, and will mention them later, the youngster has got to be made aware of the benefits of behaving well. The first thing that needs to happen is that he needs to be informed of the damage this type of antisocial behaviour can do to his relationships and career prospects. As previously mentioned, he also needs to be set manageable targets that will help him to control his outbursts. Something that has worked for me is getting the student to use a self-regulatory pro-forma, where they indicate, using notches on a five-bar gate, the number of times they have been just about to swear, but thought better of it, bit their tongues and controlled themselves. I know that the expression 'being taken for a ride' might pop into many of your heads as you read this paragraph. Yes, this system does require you to trust in the individual's wish to change their behaviour. Yes, they could abuse the system very easily. However, isn't this just the point of the exercise? It is important to put some of the onus onto the student to get them to think about the issue and to take some responsibility for their own behaviour. I would be lying if I said that I have had 100 per cent success with this method. When you take risks with students like these, there are bound to be failures. However, I usually find that most difficult youngsters are unhappy about the way they behave in lessons and are keen to do something about it. So again, I keep trying. I use these self-regulatory sheets to deal with a number of annoying habits such as students swinging on their chairs; getting out of their seats; talking across the classroom to their friends.

- **Accessing resources:** Although, when confronted, many difficult students recognize their antisocial behaviour, very few of them have the confidence to tackle their problems on their own or feel they have the resources to bring about a modification of their behaviours. Your role within these initial sessions is to convince the youngster that they do have the skills and qualities to turn things around. This is where really knowing your students comes into play. My research into the underachievement of boys revealed that, in out-of-school contexts, many of these youngsters do display many of the skills and qualities that we are desperately trying to encourage in school. Take Marc, Robert, Alistair and Colin, for example. A bigger bunch of rogues you simply couldn't ask for. These students were simply the bane of many a teacher's life. They were constantly absent or late, rarely handed work in on time, were often rude and aggressive and generally extremely uncooperative. In talking to them, however, I discovered that Marc was a ballroom dancing champion, Stuart got up at 5:45 a.m. to do a paper round, Alistair worked all day Saturdays in his dad's motor repair shop and Colin was captain of the school football team. Figure 5.2 shows an amalgamation of the skills and qualities of these four lads. I am sure you will agree that the list is quite impressive.

My advice would, therefore, be to use your meeting time to audit the student's successes, both in and out of school, to use these examples to build up their self–esteem, and to get the message across that they do have it in them to take control over their lives in school. As we know, a lack of self-esteem is very often the issue, and this type of student will struggle to come up with

Qualities	Skills
Reliability	Motor co-ordination skills
Conscientiousness	Musical skills
Perseverance and staying power	Problem-solving skills
Ability to work with others	Leadership skills
Approachability	Communication skills
Loyalty	Physical skills

Figure 5.2 Qualities and skills audit for Marc, Robert, Alistair and Colin

things they are successful at. You may, therefore, have to be highly proactive in initiating the process. Things you could focus on could be:

- a successful work experience placement
- their membership of a school or local sports team
- any community work they might do
- part-time jobs
- hobbies and interests
- outside school clubs
- drama, music and dance productions in school or in the community
- their roles within the family (e.g. do they act as carers?)

Rehearsing success: This is quite a difficult thing for many youngsters to do. The process requires them to create a visual image of how they are going to change their behaviour in school, and what life could be like if they were able to achieve it. It also requires them to internally rehearse their responses to specific classroom scenarios, and to start to think about how they can also transfer these newly found skills to other challenging situations. Through the process of modelling and role-play you can coach the youngster into acting appropriately in lessons. Let me give you a brief example of where this strategy has been implemented in my school. A number of teachers voiced their concern to the SENCO about the way a small group of youngsters behaved when they entered and exited their classrooms. These students would arrive to the lesson just a few minutes late each time – not late enough for the teacher to create a major fuss about it, but late enough to disturb the teacher's flow and to break the concentration of the other students in the class. They would come into the room and fling their bags down on the table and say something like: 'Hi, Miss, how are you? Sorry we're late Miss, we had to get a drink. What we doing today?' They would leave the room in a similarly robust manner. Although I am sure you will agree there is nothing particularly malicious about this behaviour, you will appreciate that the regularity of this occurrence was, nevertheless, both annoying and stressful to the teachers concerned. It had got to the stage where these teachers were beginning to build up an increasing level of resentment towards this group of students. The first thing the SENCO had to do was to get these youngsters to understand how their behaviour made the teachers and the rest of the students in the class actually feel. He did this by mirroring their actions and by showing them how this behaviour appeared to the other students in the class. He then asked these youngsters to talk about an activity or hobby that was important to them or to describe one of their favourite television programmes. Once the children had finished doing this, he then asked them to imagine what they would feel like if their brothers or sisters constantly interrupted their activity or programme. Having done all of this, he then booked the drama room and got the youngsters to carry out a number of role-play exercises that involved them practising, making an orderly entrance and exit to and from a classroom. Although it is fair to say that these youngsters continued to be difficult in lessons, the subject teachers reported a dramatic improvement in this specific aspect of their behaviour. I am not suggesting for one minute that you go to such lengths in your attempts to get your difficult youngsters to rehearse their newly modified responses, but I hope this example gives you an idea of the sort of thing you can do to help students change their behaviour. It is important that, when everything else has failed, it may then be the time to try a more creative approach to solving the problem.

What does a behaviour plan look like?

The answer to this question is quite simple; it is entirely up to you what your plan looks like. However, there are some guiding principles you may wish to employ when designing the final document. You need to devise a plan that identifies the student's targets clearly and that is written in language that is accessible to them. The plan must also be easy to implement and must not run for too great a time. My experience shows me that the plan will lose impact after about three weeks. The other thing you might like to do in order to give the process a degree of formality and status, is to include a student–teacher contract in your behaviour-management plan. I have provided two examples of behaviour plans you, in Figures 5.3 and 5.4, but please do not see these as being set in stone. You need to adapt your plan according to the situation and the needs of the individual student.

Although earlier we explored the intrinsic benefits to the students of behaving appropriately in lessons, this on its own is often not enough to motivate students to modify a behaviour pattern that has sometimes taken

- I have discussed my behaviour with the following members of staff:

Subject teacher	✓
Head of Department	✓
Head of Year	✓
Form Tutor	✓
Parents	

and agree that there are certain aspects of my behaviour that are not acceptable. I agree to work with them in changing my behaviour.

- **These are things I need to work on.** (To increase the student's ownership of the process they need to write this down in their own words. I have provided some examples of inappropriate behaviours for you. However be careful not to overload the student with targets)

Shouting out in class
Swinging on chair
Being out of my seat in lessons
Being rude
Losing my temper

- **How will I set about doing this?** (Again, this needs to be in 'student speak' but I have given a few examples below)

I will use my self-monitoring form to see how many times I stop myself shouting out/ swinging on my chair.

I will try to bring my own pen, pencil and ruler so I don't have to get out of my seat during lessons. If I need equipment I will ask my teacher to bring equipment over to my desk.

When I feel that I am starting to lose my temper I will take a deep breath and count slowly from ten down to one. If there is a sink in the room I will ask if I can wash my face with cold water.

- **How will my teachers help me?** (It is necessary to jointly brainstorm the way that staff could support the student. Again, I have put down a few suggestions below.)

My teacher could recognize when I am getting angry and give me some 'time out'.

My teacher could praise and encourage me when they can see I am trying to improve.

My teachers could talk to each other about how well I am doing.

- **Comment Box** (Take every opportunity to praise the student for any progress made. However, if things haven't gone to well, try to make your comments as positive as possible by writing something like – Gary struggled to meet his targets today but I am looking forward to Monday's lesson where he can give it a 'fresh go'.)

Signed:......................................Student
Signed......................................Subject Teacher
Signed......................................Head of Department *
Signed......................................Head of Year *
Signed......................................Form Tutor *
Signed......................................Parent *

* You have to decide how formal to make your plan and who to involve.

Figure 5.3 Behaviour management plan for Student X

Form Group: 9M

Area of concern: Student X has a tendency to upset and annoy his peers through use of misplaced and inappropriate comments

Area of concern in student's own words: Stop winding other students up.

Subject Teacher: Mr X   **Support by: Miss Y (TA)**   **Support began:**

Review date: 4 weeks from time of plan being initiated

Targets to be achieved	Achievement criteria	Possible resources or techniques	Possible class strategies	Ideas for TA/LSA	Outcome
To interact with others without teasing them	Reduced number of incidents in a 4 week period. In previous 4 week period 12 incidents were reported.	Mr X, Miss Y, Form Tutor and Student's mother to meet to discuss Student W's behaviour plan. Mr X to meet with Student W to mirror and model student's behaviour. Target will be set and Mr X will help Student W to rehearse more appropriate responses when talking with peers. Student W will be informed that Form Tutor, parents and TA both know about the plan. Loss of free time at morning and lunchtime break. Loss of 'computer time' at home School 's community service.	Intervene early Remind student of consequences. Seek every opportunity to praise student for meeting targets Keep a record of student's behaviour	All of the previous Talk through incidents with Student W. Mirror, model student's behaviour and ask him what he could have done differently. Rehearse alternative scenarios. Keep a record of his behaviour.	

Figure 5.4 Behaviour plan for student W

years to become established. It is imperative that you initiate a reward system. I therefore strongly advise you to:

- use plenty of verbal praise
- use the school's reward system
- inform other relevant members of staff, for example, Head of Year, Form tutor, and so on
- telephone or write to parents informing them of their child's progress
- issue privileges to the student, for example, half an hour on the computer
- use departmental funds to purchase some confectionary or a gift voucher.

I've tried everything but it's still not working!

So what happens if you feel you have tried everything? You've put a behaviour-management plan into place, you've got to know your students well, you've made particular efforts to strike up, and maintain, good relationships with your challenging youngsters, and you have set up individual behaviour plans with some, or all, of them. Despite doing all of this, however, you are still getting challenging and unacceptable behaviour from one or two students in your classes. Where do you go from here?

Perhaps one of the hardest things to accept for any conscientious teacher, but particularly for those more idealistic teachers in the dawn of their careers is that you 'can't win them all'. That is not to say you should adopt a defeatist attitude and stop trying. However, you do need to be realistic about what you are able, and are not able, to achieve in your first few years of teaching. This could, therefore, now be the time for you to pass the issue on to your Head of Department to lend some weight to the proceedings. You need to know, however, that Heads of Department and Heads of Year get extremely frustrated when members of staff abdicate responsibility for their students and when they get youngsters referred to them without these teachers making a real effort to implement the school's behaviour policy. However, if you can convince them that you really have tried absolutely everything, but that you have reached the end of the road, then I feel confident that you will receive the support and encouragement you deserve. Before you take the big step and refer these

Strategies employed	Have done
Set up and implemented a classroom and behaviour-management plan that consists of my formally setting out my own rules/routines/expectations and gradated sanctions	✓
Made maximum use of the school's assertive policy to support my discipline	✓
Made every effort to strike up good relationships out of the classroom with my more challenging students	✓
Formally interviewed these challenging students with a view to modifying their behaviour	✓
Set up, implemented and evaluated a behaviour-management plan with these youngsters	✓

Figure 5.5. Strategy checklist

students to your HOD I suggest that you document everything you have done up to the point of referral. The checklist shown in Figure 5.5 should be helpful.

You may find that a number of actions are proposed. The youngster may be removed from the class on a permanent basis, or they may be taken out of your lessons for a temporary period of time. As tempting as it may be to simply get rid of the problem I would suggest that you initially opt for the latter strategy. Providing opportunities are given to both parties to reflect on the issues in hand, this timeout period can often prove to be beneficial in helping to build bridges and re-establish your expectations. One thing I am absolutely certain of is your need to retain an element of control over proceedings. The youngster should *not* be allowed back into your class until they have agreed to meet your basic expectations. I would suggest that prior to the student being re-admitted to your lessons, you arrange a meeting with the HOY/HOD, the student and yourself and that you prepare clear written guidelines for this re-admittance. To exemplify exactly what I mean by this, I have included a transcript of a conversation I had with a Year Ten girl whom I had to temporarily exclude from my lessons for some outrageous antisocial behaviour. Again, this is not supposed to be a prescriptive list, but has been included simply as a means of illustrating the importance of maintaining an element of control in a difficult situation. It is important for a teacher to have the feeling of empowerment restored to them, especially in situations where they have felt particularly impotent.

Hannah, I would like to welcome you back to the class. I am looking forward to working with you again. You need to know, however, that if you are to make a really fresh start you need to read through and accept my behaviour expectations. It is very important for you to understand that these expectations apply not only to you but to **every other student** in the class.

It is important that you:

arrive promptly and adopt a 'low profile' when entering the room

get your working equipment/books out and wait quietly until I am ready to start the lesson

not call out in class and/or make stupid comments

sit on your own when I am giving instructions or explaining the work

(If things go well, I will allow you to sit with a student of my choice)

wait behind after the lesson to discuss anything that you are unhappy about

leave the room without arguing if I ask you to do so.

You will notice from my choice of language when outlining the conditions for readmittance, that I have been extremely specific in my expectations. Hopefully, you will be able interpolate from these expectations exactly what the nature of Hannah's anti-social behaviour was. Did Hannah become a reformed character as a result of this action? Of course she didn't. However, although she continued to be a challenging student, her behaviour was nevertheless not as extreme, and was therefore just about acceptable and certainly more containable.

In this chapter I have attempted to do a number of things. In the early part, I described what generally constitutes disruptive behaviour. I then went on to explore a number of different rationales for why some students might choose to behave in such a challenging manner. Towards the end of this chapter, I outlined a number of preventative measures you can take to help reduce the likelihood of disruptive behaviour in your lessons, before then going on to describe some supportive discipline techniques you could use when all else fails. I hope I have met the objective of the chapter, which was to provide you as beginning teachers, with 'somewhere else to go' when all your discipline strategies have failed. I leave you in the final throes of this chapter with the following message. It can take a teacher many years to reach a stage in their career where student disruption is not a major concern. Even the most experienced and skilled teachers are subject to antisocial behaviour which has a root cause well beyond their control. The message is clear: have high but realistic expectations and never stop trying!

Suggestions

- Make your expectations of the types of behaviours you find unacceptable absolutely transparent to your students. Better still, canvas the opinions of your students as to what behaviours they find to be counteractive to learning. Display this list on the noticeboard/walls

- Ensure that you reflect upon and evaluate your lessons on a daily basis, using what you learn to inform future interactions with your students

- Check the accessibility of material and language to SEN pupils with your TA on a regular basis

- Provide opportunities for your students to talk about their feelings

- Carry out a 'skills' and 'qualities' audit with some of your more unmotivated and challenging students. Doing this shows them that you recognize them for who they are and indicates to them that they are not 'useless', and that they do have something to be proud of

6 Running a successful tutor group

Morning folks. Right, settle down, trainers and coats off, shoes on, turn your chairs this way, face me – come on, let's get sorted – it's registration time. Absolute silence please. (Pause, scan the class-room.) That's excellent, thank you. Right, I have a number of things to go through before we start the PHSE lesson, so, listen quietly and carefully. By the end of the lesson I need your log books up here, please. Gemma, Richard – I need your absence notes for Monday. Craig, your mum phoned. You're to meet her in the main playground at 3:10 today – she forgot to tell you that you're booked in to see the dentist at 3:30. Martha, Mr Williams wants to see you now about the incident in Science yesterday. Hang on a minute, I'll have to write you out a pass. Andrew, can you give these letters out to the rest of the class. Oh, yes, I nearly forgot. There are nine of you who still owe me reply slips for your reports. Please bring them up here now; otherwise, you'll be staying in after school tomorrow. Laura, Sam – please don't forget that you are staying in after school this evening. Your PSHE wasn't done – remember? Aaah, that reminds me, Mrs Murphy wants me to tell you that your Work Experience letters need to be in by the 28th. If you haven't done them, you need to do these pretty quickly. If you want help then I will be in here at the end of the day. By the way, Darren, well done for your efforts in English. Let's have a look at what you have done. Aaron and Shaun, I need to see you outside for a couple minutes before we start the lesson. The rest of you are on trust while I am out of the room talking to these boys. Meanwhile, Emily, can you and Becky please give out the PSHE booklets and the exercise books so that we can make a start when I come back.

And so the tutor period begins.

As beginning teachers, many of you will already have taken on some responsibility for a tutor group, either by supporting the class tutor, or by taking sole charge of your own form. Inexperienced as you are, I am sure that you have already begun to realize what a demanding role this is, and how important the form tutor is to the lives of their students. The purpose of this chapter is to explore the role of the form tutor, which I believe to be one of the most difficult and complex jobs in the school. I am not alone in this view. Research carried out by Marland and Rogers (2004) substantiates the view that many newly qualified teachers feel that they have simply been 'thrown in the deep end' as far as their form tutoring role is concerned.

> However, newly qualified teachers invariably admit that the most dif-
> ficult and sometimes the most demoralizing aspect of staring a new
> job is working with a tutor group.

As things currently stand, trainees do not need to have an intimate knowledge of the role of a form tutor. True, some trainees shadow form tutors for a period of time, while others take on tutor groups for specific time slots during their training year. However, as this experience is not a fundamental requisite for trainees to gain Qualified Teacher Status (QTS), their knowledge and understanding of the role of the form tutor is inconsistent and is often gained on an ad hoc basis. The following words from Marland and Rogers (2004) summarize the issue extremely well: 'Often they have received little or no training at college and teaching practice experience is limited.'

It is interesting to note that many schools publicly champion the role of the form tutor and Personal, Social and Health Education (PSHE) within their curriculum and pastoral infrastructures but then do very little to combat the lack of training and/or expertize of their teaching staff. Having taught in secondary schools for over thirty years, I would certainly support the view of Marland and Rogers that there is often a mismatch between what is said and what is done. They quite rightly point out that despite issuing sound bites to the contrary that many schools fail to mention the requirements of the form tutor role to new applicants, and in many cases, the form tutor role is not even in the job description. The lack of status of form tutors is often compounded once a newly qualified teacher is appointed when there are few or no team meetings and when the PSHE material presented to them is often skimpy, non-existent or issued at the last moment. They also find that when they eventually get around to delivering PSHE units, they are often interrupted by senior staff who want to take students out of the lesson for alternative purposes. However, it is not just senior staff who fail to recognize the importance of the form tutor or the tutorial periods. There are many form tutors who themselves merely pay lip service to the role. When planning their lessons, PSHE is often the last thing on the to-do list. When delivering PSHE they do not do so with the same rigour or enthusiasm as they do when delivering their subject-based lessons. This message is often picked up by students. The following quote, again from Marland and Rogers, makes the point well: 'It's funny how teachers make out the tutorial periods important but then don't do anything about it'. Secondary school student

There is no doubt in my mind that a good form tutor needs to be multi-skilled, flexible, physically and mentally robust, and comfortable adopting an authoritative and democratic teaching style, such as that described in Chapter Two. As an experienced teacher, even I found it difficult to quantify everything I did as a form tutor. I only know that, having carried out a mountain of tasks in such a short space of time, I very often came out of registration sessions and PSHE lessons absolutely shell-shocked. The process of writing this book has afforded me the opportunity to step back and to think about the role of the form tutor in more detail. In doing this, I have come up with a number of broad job-description categories, which I have placed in order of importance. However, I need to say that the status of each individual category can vary according to the perspective of the school's head teacher. My head teacher at the time of my retirement, for example, saw the role of the pastoral system within the school as being mainly there to support the academic development of the students. I, on the other hand, saw the pastoral system as being there in its own right and, as you can see below, have put this at the top of my list.

The roles of the form tutor

- To provide formal and informal opportunities for the personal and social development of students
- To provide an infrastructure to support the school's ethos on behaviour and attitudes

- To support students' academic progress

- To act as a conduit for communications between school and home

Figure 6.1 shows the full extent of your role as a form tutor. Looks onerous doesn't it? Don't panic! It is my intention to work systematically through the four categories offered above and to offer guidance and advice on a number of issues associated with these specific form tutoring roles.

Providing formal and informal opportunities for the personal and social development of your students

I wonder how many of you have actually thought about what the ultimate aim of a good form tutor is. Allow me to share this view with you. I feel that the form tutor's overriding aim should be to create well-balanced, socially and morally competent students, who are able to realize their full learning potential and lead happy lives. Figure 6.1 shows how this can be done. Although this may sound rather idealistic, my premise is that if you begin your career with this view in mind, you will at least start off on the right track. Believe you me, you will not get all of it right all of the time, but at least you will be clear about the route which you wish to take with your students.

At the beginning of each year with my form group, I made sure that I reinforced my rules, routines and expectations. I also referred them to the illustrated model shown in Figure 6.2 which I used to explain my form tutoring role to the students. The model has been adapted and much simplified from the work on personality by psychologist Sigmund Freud.

I explained to my students that my role was to be responsible for taking them from the 'id' stage of their personality through to the 'superego' stage. I told them that the id stage relates to the side of their personality that has a tendency to simply take what it wants. This behaviour is typical of most young children, but can also be seen in many older youngsters. The person at this stage of their lives does not have a fully developed conscience.

Moving on, I then went on to explain that the 'ego' stage represents the part of us that motivates us to commit an immoral act if we think we are unlikely to get caught. This is the stage that most youngsters in your tutor group will be in. That is, they know the broad difference between right

Supporting academic progress:

- Checking homework diaries

- Rewarding academic achievement

- Checking and reporting on academic progress

- Contacting parents on academic matters

- Target setting

- Supporting subject tutors

- Contacting parents about academic matters.

Supporting the school's stance on attitudes and behaviour:

- Acting as a mouthpiece for the school's behaviour and attitude policy. Clarifying and implementing school rules

- Supporting school's policy on punctuality, attendance and uniform

- Rewarding good behaviour through credit system

- Imposing sanctions on students who contravene school rules., e.g. giving detentions, contacting parents.

Aiding communication between school and home:

- Distributing letters to go home to parents

- Collecting reply slips

- Passing on information to students.

Supporting child on an individual basis:

- Counselling students experiencing difficulties

- Helping to 'move students on'

- Referring students to other people/organizations.

Supporting the personal and social development of the students:

- Teaching Personal and Health Education

- Organizing form trips and events

- Chairing form meetings

- Collecting monies for charity events.

Figure 6.1 The role of the form tutor

and wrong but, given the opportunity, they will go ahead and make some questionable moral decisions at times.

Finally, the ultimate goal – the superego stage, represents the truly moral being where a person has obtained a fully developed conscience and where true altruism reigns.

Of course, it is not as simple as this. I explained to the students that humans are complex beings and that these stages in our personal, social and moral development are by no means clearly defined. It is important for students to realize that, even as adults, the id sometimes tends to prevail, and we start to behave selfishly when we don't get our own way. I then went on to explain to them that sometimes it is the ego which tends to dominate our behaviour, and that we often do things we know to be wrong, only ceasing this behaviour when we know we are likely to get caught. As form tutors, you need to think about this before you start to take the moral high ground with your students when admonishing them for their misdemeanours. For example, how many times, when you have been speeding, have you slowed down when you have spotted a police car? How many times have you taken the odd roll of sticky tape from work? How many times have you told a lie to get yourself out of a tricky situation? The list is endless.

Of course, the superego comes into play with some people more than others. Most of us at times are capable of carrying out altruistic acts, where the only reward is simply knowing that we have done the right thing. Although I am no psychologist, I found that this simple model helped to outline my aims to my tutor group. I also used this model several times with some particularly challenging and self-centred students in the past. I know that it helped these youngsters to understand their behaviour and to rectify some of their more selfish traits for the benefit of the other students in the class. Try it, and see what you think!

It is fair to say that many form tutors fail to recognize that they have a major role to play in the moral education of their students, and the notion of adopting the strategy outlined above is likely to be totally alien to their way of thinking. These form tutors are absolutely fine when it comes to issuing House Rules to the class but are reluctant, and often not skilled enough to be able to explore the moral perspective of many of these rules. I would urge you as new form tutors to take every opportunity to interweave ethical issues into your everyday interactions with students, taking care not to create major moral issues where there are none. The following words by Marland and Rogers (2004) clarify this process extremely well:

> How he or she handles the details from attendance to communications with home, from behavioural discussions to checking homework will bring the details of the school injunctions to relate to the

Baby annoyed at not getting what it wants – Id Stage

Boy feeding dog under the table knowing that he is 'breaking the rules' but being prepared to try to get away with it. 'Ego' stage.

Youngster showing 'altruistic' tendencies – 'Superego' stage.

Figure 6.2 Cartoons for Freud Text

higher, longer-term ideals: explanations of why we need a fire drill; advice to the student who was rude to another teacher; a discussion of how to react to and make use of critical comments by a teacher on a piece of work. Every episode is handled not only for itself but also, with varied emphasis, as a lesson for the longer term.

Having said all this, if you do not practise what you preach you are highly unlikely to make any impact upon the way your students think or behave. Although it is somewhat dated, the research by McPhail et al. (1972) is still highly valuable in showing that many adolescents confirmed that they felt little changed by advice on how to behave if those giving it did not embody that advice in their ways of relating to their students in their teaching. Leading by example is therefore the best way to get your point across. For example, if you continually arrive late for your tutor period, how an earth can you chastise a student for being late to registration or to their lessons? This quote from Michael Rutter's work on the upbringing of children demonstrates the potency of leading by example: 'Children show a marked tendency to "model" their behaviour on that of those whom they love, trust and respect.'

In Chapter Four, I briefly explored the functions of the reptilian brain and described how our knowledge of this part of the brain can relate to our classroom practice. I am in no doubt whatsoever that understanding how the reptilian brain and the limbic system works can most certainly help you to become a better form tutor. As we know, the reptilian brain is the primeval part of the brain that is responsible for routine body functions which operate continually outside our conscious awareness – such as breathing, heart beat, blood pressure, temperature, balance and so on. It is also responsible for our survival responses – for example, the fight-or-flight response in the face of danger. This is the part of the brain that seeks physical and emotional security. Students need somewhere and someone to run to when things go badly for them. Creating a form base that is bright, comfortable and secure from outside threat is an important role for the form tutor. Simply controlling who comes into your form room at break and lunchtimes, and making yourself available to these youngsters when they need you, can really enhance your relationships with your students.

Shaw and Hawes (1998) explain how we all have a predisposition towards social conformity – including hierarchies and pecking orders. Despite thousands of years of evolution, we still conform to rote and ritual. Hopefully you will now begin to fully understand the need to establish rules and routines during your registration and PSHE sessions. By doing so, you will be providing these youngsters with the security needed for *real* learning to take place.

The limbic system is the part of the brain that concerns itself with governing our emotions, and it lies at the very heart of our beliefs, values and sense of identity. It is also important to note that this part of the brain contains our long-term memory. As we saw in Chapter One, the more a teacher engages the emotions of a student, the more likely it is that the material is will be embedded in the long-term memory. of the child, and the quicker and easier it will be to recall. Obviously, having this knowledge is imperative for subject teachers, but it is also very important for teachers carrying out a pastoral role.

So, how, in practical terms, can we utilize our knowledge of the brain to develop our relationships with our students? The first thing to suggest is that you endeavour to create a corporate sense of identity within your tutor group. Build up the notion that this is the best form in the year group and try to create a sense of pride and privilege of being a member of this class. You can do this in a number of ways. Take every opportunity to take your students out on form trips. It doesn't have to be far, nor does it have to be over-ambitious. You could take them to the local swimming pool and for a burger at a nearby fast-food restaurant. If you live in a town with a professional football team, you could get cheap booking rates and take them to see a match. Other things you could do would be to take them ice/roller skating, paintballing or you could take them to a local theme park or to see a show. Quite honestly, it doesn't really matter what you do because the youngsters will simply enjoy being out with each other and with you! I have found that taking students out on form trips, especially in Year Seven, has proved to be a major investment in helping me to build up good relationships with my tutor group. There have been times, later on in their school careers, when I have had to get quite 'heavy' with some of these youngsters, and I am convinced that it was all the hard work carried out earlier on, that created an infrastructure of trust between us, and that allowed these students to accept this discipline with good grace. I also never cease to be amazed at what I learn about my youngsters during the many informal chats I have with them on these trips. For example, I found out recently that Andrew, Ben and Peter all played the guitar, that Helen trained with the England netball team, and that Samantha took part in amateur theatrical productions. This has resulted in me continually renegotiating my image of these youngsters.

Building up happy memories for students is a vital part of form tutoring. One of the things I did with my last tutor group was to produce a scrapbook of memories for each of the years they have been with me. This scrapbook comprised photographs I took of my youngsters at school, on trips and local newspaper cuttings that relate to my students. It was very rewarding to see many of my students flicking through the pages of these books during break or registration and recalling the fun times they had in earlier years. They were certainly a topic of conversation and did a lot to create that all important team spirit and sense of unity within the tutor group. At the end of the five years, I did two things: first, I carried out a free raffle draw so that five students could each take one year book home with them; second, I invited parents and students in to attend a special commemorative evening for my tutor group. I scanned the photographs in the scrapbook and presented these in slide form in a PowerPoint presentation as part of an evening of celebration and farewell to my tutor group.

Another thing you can do is to find out when your youngsters are taking part in school sports or musical/drama productions. Just turning up to watch these students means a tremendous amount to them and helps to create that all important bond required for a successful tutor group. Whether *you* do this with *your* tutor group is not the issue. The whole point of my telling you what I did with my form is to get you to think about what you can do to create a sense of identity within your own tutor group.

In Chapter Four, and in *Managing Your Classroom* (2007), I discuss at length the effect of the physical layout of the classroom on the mood and behaviour of the students. There has been a great deal of research to show how the layout and condition of the classroom can have a marked effect on the work ethic, behaviour and attitudes of students. This effect should not be underestimated! If you take care of your surroundings and encourage your students to do the same, you will go a long way to creating a positive ethos and sense of pride in your classroom.

Obviously, one of the main aims of any form tutor is to get to know your students. Take time to talk to each and every one of them on an individual basis to find out what makes them tick. Keep records of your conversations and of the things they do out of school. Talk to the youngsters about their hobbies and interests and take the time to show an interest in them as people. You could use a questionnaire to act as a focus for discussion. Try not to restrict your conversations to the most approachable members of your form. Make an effort to involve all students in your group activities. Keep your eyes open and pay attention to detail. Most students really like it when you comment on their contributions to school life. It illustrates that you have noticed them and their achievements. You do, however, need to be very aware of the issue of disclosure, and it is absolutely vital that you warn your students that you may have to pass on sensitive information to their HOY or to another appropriate adult.

I have expounded in some detail the need to create a sense of well-being and security in your tutor group. All this is fine, but remember that your job as a teacher is to find ways to 'move these youngsters on'. As a form tutor, you need to constantly find opportunities to challenge your students emotionally and socially. In order to do this, you need to get to know your students very well. Knowing when to challenge them and when to simply let things be, is an integral part of form tutoring. The following quote from an unknown source summarizes the skill needed to maintain a balanced approach towards your youngsters: 'Taking a class is like playing a salmon – a slight change of direction here, a discreet tightening of the line there, and so on. If you are too insensitive, you will not only break the line but lose the fish as well.'

To establish real class unity, it is important to avoid students being polarized into cliques. Make sure that, on occasions, you mix your students up during PSHE lessons. They may not be entirely happy to start with, but if you do this early enough in Year Seven they will become socialized into accepting this procedure as the norm.

Knowing when to step in is a very important skill and only you can determine when, and whether, to intervene in social issues that arise between your students. One of the main threats to a harmonious tutor group is the damage caused by rumour and gossip. I felt so strongly about this that I displayed a poster in my classroom with the following slogan on: *The most dangerous thing in the world is gossip!*

As form tutors you do have a duty to reduce conflict within your classroom and to help the students to deal with gossip and rumour-mongering. My advice would be to try to get the youngsters to sort things out for themselves first, but if this fails you need to take on a mediating or troubleshooting role. However, you must remember to remain objective and to be very careful not to get embroiled in the issue. While in the throes of writing this book I was in my dentist's waiting room flicking through a coverless magazine when I came across a story that I thought would be very useful in helping my youngsters deal with hurtful gossip, rumour and hearsay. As you will see, the story refers to something called the Triple Filter Test.

A Socratic lesson

In ancient Greece, Socrates was famous for holding the pursuit of knowledge in the highest esteem. One day a man bumped into him and said: 'Socrates, let me tell you what I heard about your friend'.

> 'First', Socrates replied, "I'd like you to pass the Triple Filter Test. Take a moment to filter what you are about to say. The first filter is truth. 'Are you sure what you heard is true'?

'No', the man said. 'Actually I just heard about it and . . .'.

'So, you don't know whether it is true or not', Socrates replied. 'Now let's try the filter of goodness. Is what you're about to say about my friend something good'?

'No, on the contrary'.

'So', Socrates continued, 'you want to tell me something bad, but you're not certain it's true. You may still pass the test though. Lastly, there's the filter of usefulness. Is what you are going to tell me going to be useful to me'?

'No, not really'.

'Well', concluded Socrates, 'if what you want to say isn't true, good or useful, then why would you want to tell me at all'?

This is why Socrates was a great philosopher and held in such high esteem. It also explains why he never found out his friend was having a relationship with his wife!

Once the laughter had died down, I used this story to illustrate to the students how to deal with rumour, hearsay and gossip. Whenever I heard of my students spreading gossip or half-truths I referred them to the following poster on my wall and asked them to think long and hard about what they are saying and doing, and whether they would pass the Triple Filter Test:

Is what you are saying

True?

Good?

Useful?

Would you pass the Triple Filter Test?

One of the hardest things I have ever had to do in my role as form tutor was to try to pick up the pieces after students had been feuding with each other over a long period of time. In these situations, it was very important for me to remain neutral, and to let each party know that I believed both of them to be sincere about their perceptions of the issues that lay at the heart of the conflict. I used the term 'perceptions' because this is exactly what they are. Each person will have his or her own social construction of the truth, and no matter how hard you try, you may ultimately have to accept that you will never be able to get one student to fully understand the perspective of the other.

You need to be able to talk your youngsters through these issues and get them to rehearse ways of avoiding situations that might lead to further conflict. Allow me to share with you one such situation that occurred with a girl who was in my Year Nine tutor group. Let's call this youngster Maria.

Maria and another girl, let's call her Kim, had been experiencing serious problems with each other for nearly a year. It finally got to the point where the two of them ended up scrapping like alley cats in public. The issue was referred to the HOY who ended up getting the two sets of parents together to discuss the matter. No matter what the HOY suggested to help these youngsters solve the problem, nothing was resolved, and the situation soon reached an impasse. It was obvious to me that, unless something was done pretty quickly, we would soon have another fight on our hands. All it was going to take was a look or a passing comment by one or both of the girls and we would have two school exclusions on our hands. I took Maria out of one of her lessons and spent half an hour rehearsing a number of strategies that would help her to cope when she met up with Kim again. I took the opportunity to actually model some acceptable and unacceptable responses. This was an important thing to do because, as we have already seen, body language, voice tone and degree of eye contact are all important elements in helping to reduce or to inflame conflict. The text below provides the basis of a letter I wrote to Maria's mother and HOY outlining to them what action I had taken on the matter.

I have spoken to Maria at length about the incident that happened after school yesterday and have suggested a number of strategies she could use to cope in conflict situations such as these. I realize that in expecting her to deal successfully with this type of situation, I am asking a lot of a 13-year-old. I have told Maria that if she manages to gain these skills by the time she is an adult, she will have done extremely well. I have to say that Maria was extremely positive about the whole process and is willing to 'give it a go'.

- Keep your facial expression and body language as 'neutral' as possible. Do not sneer, do not 'look down your nose' at the other person.

- Give yourself and the other person time and space to consider the issue and to think about the other person's perspective. You could say something like: 'We are both angry, give me some time to think about what you are saying'. **NEVER** try to deal with issues when you are angry; it will only make things worse. Walk away!

- Get rid of the audience! They will only make things worse and you will find it difficult to 'back down' in public.

- If things are bad and you need an adult to act as a 'negotiator' then come and see me.

- Accept that there will always be 'personality conflicts'. If you don't get on – accept it, be pleasant to each other, but

- Don't keep going back for more!

- Accept that you will not get things right every time.

- Avoiding conflict takes a lot of skill and maturity – you will not acquire these skills overnight!

The very best of luck Maria!

Maria and her mum were very pleased with the practical advice offered, and I am happy to report that, apart from one or two 'hiccups', Maria was very successful in avoiding conflict with Kim over the final two years of their secondary school careers.

You will remember that in Chapter Three, I described the need for teachers to continually be reflective about their teaching. I would, again, urge you to constantly evaluate your role as form tutor. Don't be afraid to canvass the opinions of your students, but do so in the wider context of the whole group working together to explore ways to improve the smooth running of the form. And, once again, do not become despondent if things do not always go smoothly. As with subject teaching, if you get things right 80 per cent of the time I would deem this as real success.

Providing an infrastructure to support the school's behaviour and attitudes policy

In my role as Professional Development Tutor, I often sat on interview panels whose responsibility it was to appoint NQTs to the school. One of my head teacher's favourite questions was to ask the candidates to define the role of the form tutor. Most candidates were able to come up with responses that generally related to the form tutor's role in supporting their students both pastorally and academically, but very few were able to deliver the answer he was really looking for: that the form tutor should act as a conduit for the transference of the beliefs, values and attitudes of the school.

Every school should have a behaviour/attitudes policy and it is very important for you as beginning teachers to understand your role in helping to implement this. You can do this at the beginning of the year when you go through the school rules with your students. No one is asking you to agree with all the rules, but what is absolutely imperative is that you do your utmost to present a cohesive and unified approach to the students by implementing these rules fairly and consistently.

All too often I hear struggling teachers bemoaning the fact that discipline in the school has 'really gone down the drain' and how the 'management' needs to do something about it. As far as I am concerned, they have missed the point. Each and every one of us has a responsibility to impart the values, norms and expectations of the school to the students we meet during the school day. It is important for us to remember that a strong school is a school where staff all work together to meet a common aim – a chain will always break at its weakest link. The message is simple – do not become that weakest link!

So, what exactly can you do to make a full contribution to the ethos of the school? I am suggesting that you start to consider your tutor periods and your PSHE lessons as microcosms of the school community and that you use these to promote a positive ethos among the students in your tutor group. If students leave your registration session not having been given the right messages for the day, and in the wrong frame of mind then, quite simply, the buck stops with you! You will appreciate, therefore, how important it is to get your registrations and PSHE lessons right as far as classroom and behaviourmanagement issues are concerned.

The following from Ian Startup (2003), an Advanced Skills Teacher in a large comprehensive school, makes the point in an extremely apposite manner: 'form tutors make too little use of time devoted to registration periods to induct students into their next session of lessons'.I write at length in *Managing Your Classroom* (2007) about the need to set up clear rules, routines and expectations with students. The registration session is the ideal opportunity for you to set up your students for the day. The first thing you need to do is to call for silence. I liked to use a countdown system from three down to one because it gave the youngsters a brief moment to finish what they are saying. However, once I was ready to take the register then the rule is simple; silence must prevail. I would be an absolute liar if I said that this system was foolproof. Youngsters did try it on, and did try to have a crafty word with their neighbours while I was taking the register. In order to cater for this, I had a slogan which I referred to at the beginning of every registration session; 'Quiet or clear up'. What this meant was that if I caught a student talking during the registration process, they knew that they were going to have to join me at the end of the day to help to clear up my classroom. Call it 'community service' if you like. Some of you reading this might possibly think that this approach might have been a little over the top. However, as I stressed in *Managing Your Classroom*, if a teacher wants to establish and maintain good order in the classroom, there is a need for them to gain a psychological edge over the youngsters in their classes. In my opinion, here we had a situation which was absolutely shouting out for the implementation of firm rules and routines. To be strictly honest, any teacher will tell you that you don't actually need silence to take a register. You could simply scan the room and place a tick or a nought in the attendance box without the students even being aware that you are doing this. So why make a big deal about getting the youngsters quiet? I feel that obtaining silence is important for a number of reasons. In my registration sessions, I asked the students to take their coats off, to put their school shoes on, to sit down on a chair, to face the front of the class and to make eye contact with me while I am taking the register. Doing this conveyed the message to the students that it is me, and not them, who determined what happens in my classroom. I also felt that by imposing some sense of order at the beginning of the day, I was doing my bit to support my colleagues who came across these students later on during the school day. Finally, because I was legally bound to produce accurate attendance records for the Local Authority (LA), I needed to make sure I did not make mistakes when I was taking the register. Mistakes can happen easily in a noisy classroom.

I have explained how implementing the advice given above can benefit the ethos of the school, but surely, this book is all about getting on with teenagers and improving their learning! The question you may be asking, however, is how did this affect my relationships with students? The answer is simple. You read in Chapter Three how perceptive and demanding the students were of their teachers. Despite often giving off signals to the contrary, most youngsters know what is right. They demand and expect their teachers to impose a sense of order on them at a time in their lives when they sometimes struggle to understand facets of their own behaviour, and/or when they find it difficult to control themselves. In short, they want their teachers to act as their consciences until such time as they can fully exercise their own. What many teachers fail to understand is that the role of the form tutor is essential in helping to contribute to the ethos and culture of the school. The words of Ian Startup (2003) again make my point extremely well: 'OFSTED observed of a failing school that 'little is done by staff to define and secure a distinctive and appropriate school culture.'

There will be occasions when students are reported to you for misbehaving in other lessons. You will have to strike that fine balance between supporting your students and supporting the member of staff who has complained to you. Very often, in situations such as these, the truth lies somewhere between the two perspectives, and you will have to steer a careful course, making sure that both parties feel they have been justly treated. If it is obvious, however, that your youngster has simply been out of order, you need to follow up on their bad behaviour. I would suggest that in cases of repeated misbehaviour, you support your colleagues by issuing your own sanctions. It is, of course, equally important to reward instances of good or improved behaviour, and you can do that through the school's formal reward process or by using your own system.

Providing academic support for your students

How can you as beginning teachers and form tutors support the academic progress of the students in your tutor group? The first thing I would advise you to do is to gather evidence to help you provide an academic profile of the students. Using prior-assessment data, which usually contain such information as reading and maths scores, SAT results and, in some cases, information about the learning styles of the individuals concerned, you need to build up a central set of records. You could store this material either on a data-base on your laptop, or you could simply use a hardback folder. What is absolutely vital, however, is that you always have this data to hand when you need to make informed decisions about the youngsters in your class. It is, for example, always very useful to have this data when dealing with parents at consultation evenings.

Long before the first progress checks and/or reports are issued, you will begin to get an inkling of the students in your class who are underachieving. Informal conversations in the staffroom with subject staff often reveal a lot about the way things are going for some of your students. Sometimes subject tutors will write to you formally informing you of their concern for individuals in your classes. Do not ignore these early warnings. My advice to you here would be to follow up on this by sending out a 'round robin' circular to find out whether similar patterns of under-achievement or misbehaviour are occurring in other subject areas. It is important, however, to make sure that you study the prior assessment data before you interview the child. Having this data available will help you to make a judgment as to whether these teachers have realistic expectations of this youngster. After weighing up the situation, you might find out that the youngster is simply unable to cope with the work being set, and this may be the message you are going to have to convey to his subject teachers. Talking with, rather than to, the youngster will give you a clearer indication of the nature of the problem and help you both to move the situation on. However, it may turn out that the student is underachieving across the board and that something does need to be done about it. Many form tutors, at this stage, might be tempted to simply inform their HOY and leave things at that. I need to stress very strongly that, at this stage, *you* rather than the HOY, are the best person to deal with the issue. Obviously, you need to keep them fully informed, and to seek advice from them on a regular basis, but *you* see this student on a daily basis and have a much more intimate knowledge of what makes the youngster tick. Making an investment now will do absolute wonders for your relationship, not only with this student, but also with the other members of the class. I would then suggest that you offer to take on the mentoring of this individual for a specific period of time. Don't panic, this does not necessarily have to be an onerous task. All it would involve would be meeting the youngster on a regular basis – say, once a half term, reviewing the comments made by subject staff, and then setting targets for the individual concerned. Very often, youngsters, no matter how bright they are, do not know *how* to learn, and you could use some of the interview time to discuss learning strategies with them. With the HOY's permission you should try to involve the child's parents in the process to make sure that everybody is 'singing from the same hymn sheet' and co-operating with each other to support for the youngster. Parents may also like to contribute to the process by helping their children to organize their time efficiently and by offering external rewards to the youngsters for making good progress. Whatever the outcome, the one thing I am absolutely sure about is that, by doing this, your relationship with that student and their parents will dramatically improve.

I have described what you could do for individual students who, because of their poor achievement or behaviour record, have had their names brought to your notice. It is, vital, however, that you carry out this academic monitoring process with *all* of the students in your class. You need to spend some time gaining an overview of student performance by reviewing their progress checks and subject reports. Try to make it your policy to interview each student as often as possible to find out how things are going. Using the strategies described above, try to help the youngster by suggesting learning strategies and by setting them individual targets.

Homework is always a contentious issue, with parents and students alike. You can certainly play your part in helping the students to adopt a positive and organized approach towards their homework by checking homework diaries on a regular basis.

What I tended to do was to give my youngsters a two-day window to bring their homework diaries in for me to sign. My rule was simple – if the logbook was not signed by parents and presented to me within this two-day slot, then the student attended a twenty-minute detention session at lunchtime. Those of you starting with more senior tutor groups might struggle to impose such a system, especially if their previous form tutor has not bothered too much about this, but it will be a lot easier for you to realize your expectations with younger students. What is absolutely vital, however, is that you are consistent in your expectations and that you always carry out your sanctions without fail. I have to say that this is a lot easier said than done. At the beginning of this chapter, I described the first five minutes or so of a tutor period. When you are tired and absolutely 'rushed off your feet', you will find it tempting to opt out of this system, but if you do give up on this process, you will not be able to recoup the situation at a later date. If you are consistent and fair in your approach with these younger students, you will experience very little opposition to the system as the students move up into the senior school. The students will have been socialized into your rules, routines and expectations and will see the process as simply being part and parcel of being in your form.

Acting as a conduit for communications between school and home

As their form tutor, you are responsible for making sure that the students and their parents know what is going on. This means insisting that letters are taken home and that reply slips are returned for each and every student in your charge. As with my system of collecting in homework diaries or logbooks, I gave my students a deadline for returning their reply slips. Failure to meet these deadlines simply meant that these youngsters had to do 'community service' at the end of the day. As a result, I had the tidiest classroom in the school.

So, having read this chapter, the two big questions you need to ask yourself is what kind of form tutor are you now, and what kind of form tutor do you want to be? Figure 6.3 is a simple checklist that will help to inform your decision.

As a further means of helping you develop your skills as a form tutor I have presented two potential dilemmas below for you to explore. You could

Do you arrive on time for registration?	
Do you arrive well-prepared?	
Do you respect your students?	
Do you expect to receive respect from your students?	
Do you treat your students as individuals?	
Do you smile and greet the students?	
Do you utilize the students' problems as opportunities to 'move them on' socially, emotionally, academically?	
Are you a good listener?	
Do you set high standards?	
Do you apply rules and routines consistently?	
Do you use punishment sparingly?	
Do you avoid blanket punishments?	
Do you deal with the misbehaviour of your students in other classes?	
Do you extend and motivate your students?	
Do you enjoy the company of your tutor group?	
Do you really know your students well?	
Do you display your students' work?	
Do you look for ways to avoid confrontation?	
Do you avoid humiliating students?	
Do you avoid sarcasm?	
How did you fare?	

Figure 6.3 What kind of form tutor are you/will you be?

either do this on an individual basis or get together with colleagues to discuss the issues.

Dilemma 1

One student in tutor group has been given a detention by their subject teacher for failing to complete a piece of homework. Despite the student protesting (given that the reason for non-completion was a family trauma), this failed to impress the teacher concerned. The student came to me expecting me to get him off the detention. I knew that the family trauma was genuine but also that the student had a track record of missing deadlines. I also knew that the teacher concerned always adopted a black and white approach to every issue, big and small. What would you do?

This is what I did:

a) I told the student that the detention would be done (but with me, and not the teacher concerned).

b) I explained to the student that it was his track record that had let him down on occasions, *not* the actual offence in question. I kept the student for 35 minutes and not the full hour.

c) I kept the teacher informed of what I had intended to do and negotiated the reduction in time. I also hinted that it sometimes helps to talk to colleagues with a view to understanding what motivates/causes students to react/behave in particular ways.

Dilemma 2

A member of staff in your department comes to you and tells you that a member of your form has stolen his fountain pen. He is irate and assures me that through a process of deduction and elimination, he has come to the conclusion that it must have been one of my tutor group who had stolen the pen. He lambastes you in the staff room about this. **What could you do?**

This is what I did:

I listened carefully to the teacher, asked them for their side of the story and told them that I heard what they were saying. I then told them I would talk to my tutor group about this matter as soon as possible.

I spoke to my tutor group at the next registration period and told them that unless the pen turned up I would have to inform the HOY. When speaking to them I scanned the classroom making an appropriate amount of eye contact with each student.

Having explained my dilemma I appealed to the better natures of my students by asking the culprit to leave the pen where I could easily find it at the end of the day. As an alternative strategy I suggested that if anybody in the class knew who had taken the pen, they were to write the culprit's name down on a piece of paper and place it on my desk at some point during the day.

To be honest, the chances of the pen turning up are slim, but I do have to say that this strategy did work for me.

Suggestions

- You could build up a series of portraits of the students in your form. Students could produce their own personal fact sheets that could be displayed in your classroom
- A brief complimentary comment on a youngster's performance in a school play, on the football pitch or for a good piece of work they have done, goes a long way to making them feel good. Be careful where and how you praise the student as you could embarrass the student if your comments are too public
- On occasions you should try to create mixed ability and mixed gender groupings. You could also group your students according to their preferred learning styles. Perhaps you could produce some ready made name cards that can easily be placed on the desk before the students arrive to your lesson. A fun way of grouping your students is to randomly distribute playing cards. Students holding the same cards all sit and work together for that lesson
- Encourage the students to bring their own posters in for display. Display students' work they have done in other subjects: for example, artwork, poetry, ICT assignments. Use bright paper to cover display boards. Wallpaper borders make effective surrounds. Plants often lend a calming effect. Make sure that you establish a form noticeboard. You also need to appoint form monitors. ESTABLISH A FORM IDENTITY
- You might like to put aside some time a week when members of your form can simply come and chat with you. You might like to tell them when your Duty Day is so that they can walk with you and have a chat

Conclusion

I wrote this book because of my strong interest in all issues relating to classroom life. In a previous publication (*Managing Your Classroom* 2007), I focused mainly on the technical aspects of behaviour management, offering readers a whole range of tactical strategies designed to get their students to behave in lessons. Important as these strategies are, they are not enough on their own to produce motivated, well-rounded, happy students, who are keen to learn, and willing to be reflective about themselves as social and moral beings. This book has taken things a stage further, by looking at the ways in which good and bad teachers interact with students. It explores the consequences of these interactions and offers the reader a range of strategies designed to help improve teacher-student relationships.

I believe that this book is of real practical value, not only to beginning teachers, but to all those who have taken the time to read it. In the introductory chapter, I explained to you that my remit was to write about 'real' teachers, 'real' teenagers and 'real' learning scenarios. As far as possible, this book has been evidence-based, drawing on both my primary and secondary research data, as well as on my own experiences in the classroom. It was my intention to keep the theoretical side to a minimum and to provide you with practical advice and guidance about how to cope with a range of typical classroom scenarios. I hope you feel that I have realized this intention.

As you will no doubt have noted, there is a strong theme of 'reflective practice' running throughout this book. It is important to stress yet again, that the ideas and strategies offered are not to be seen as prescriptive. These methods have worked well for me over the years but it is up to you to adapt and temper these to suit your own personality, teaching style and the needs of your students. Although I am confident that I have furnished you with a number of potentially workable strategies that will help to improve your relationships with students, what I hope I have done, is to get you to ask the right questions. The fundamental tenet behind these questions should be that of establishing mutual respect and rapport with the students in your classes so that real learning can take place.

How exactly do you evaluate and quantify the quality of your relationships with your students? This is certainly a difficult task. I wrote in Chapter Three about the need for you to canvass the opinions of youngsters about your teaching. By doing this, you will be able to gain some idea of their reactions to you and your teaching style. However, it is fair to say that much of the time your assessment will be intuitive. It won't be long before you get a pretty good idea of what your students think of you. You will know this by observing their everyday responses and the way they behave in your company. You will also know if the students trust you, for example, whether they chat to you or ask for advice. However, be careful about courting popularity and remember to be true to your principles and beliefs. I mentioned in Chapter Five that the prime purpose of the teacher is not to be liked, but to improve the quality of their students' learning, and this should be done within a climate of mutual respect. Having said all this, if you can realize this aim and be popular, too, what more could you possibly want from your job?

Finally, I want to remind you how much potential influence you have over these young people. Chapters One and Three are a testimony to this. You should look upon your role as a privilege and take your responsibilities seriously. I want to conclude with a story about one of my ex-students. Let's call her Sonia. When Sonia first came into my tutor group, she was a shy little thing with really low self-esteem. Her distinct lack of confidence meant that she was very much affected by the views and opinions of the other children in the class and, as a consequence, she made very few autonomous decisions.

While driving the mini-bus back from a Year Seven form trip to a local roller skating rink, I struck up a conversation with Sonia and her friends. I mentioned how far I felt that she had come over the past year, but then told her that I felt she still needed to take a lot more risks. She wholeheartedly agreed. Then, in jest, I gave her the following challenge: During the Leavers' Assembly in Year Eleven, she was to put on a pair of Wellington boots and walk onto the stage in front of the 300 or so students, and then place a bucket over her head. We all laughed at the idea, and I then forgot about our conversation.

Well, you've guessed it! Four years later, I was standing at the back of the hall during the Leavers' Assembly, when the HOY announced that Sonia had a surprise for Mr Dixie. To my astonishment and great pride, up walked Sonia in her Wellington boots with bucket in hand. She made her way to the centre of the stage, and in a loud, confident and assertive voice, informed the audience of the challenge I had offered her four years previously. With that, she picked up the bucket and placed it firmly on her head. She left the stage to the rapturous applause of the audience. This was one of my proudest moments in teaching! I hope that the strategies offered in this book enable you to experience many such moments.

References

Aarons, M. and Gittens, T. (2001) *The Handbook of Autism*. London: Routledge.

Arsham, H. (2010) 'Educator as a midwife'. http://home.ubalt.edu/ntsbarsh/online.html#rwhatEdu [accessed 25/12/2010].

Bennett, T. (2010) *The Behaviour Guru*. London: Continuum.

Bentham, S. (2006) *A Teaching Assistant's Guide to Managing Behaviour*. Abingdon: Routledge.

Capel, S., and Heilbronn, R. (2004) *Starting to Teach in the Secondary School*. Abingdon: RoutledgeFalmer.

Dixie, G. (1998) 'Free speech', in *First Appointments*, UK, Times Educational Supplement, 23 October.

—. (2000) 'A room you can call your own', in *First Appointments*, UK, Times Educational Supplement, 27 October.

—. (2007) *Managing Your Classroom*. London: Continuum.

—. (2009) *The Trainee Secondary Teacher's Handbook*. London: Continuum.

—. (2011) *The Ultimate Teaching Manual*. London: Continuum.

Dlugokinski, M. (2010) 'ADHD made simple'. www.adhd-made-simple.com/ [accessed 24 December 2010].

Furlong, J., and Maynard, T. (1995) *Mentoring Student Teachers: The Growth of Professional Knowledge*. London: Routledge.

Garner, P. (2004) 'Challenging behaviour in the classroom in Capel', in Sheillbronn, R., Leask, M., and Turner, T. (eds), *Starting to Teach in the Secondary School*. Abingdon: RoutledgeFalmer.

Gilbert, I. (2002) *Essential Motivation in the Classroom*. London: RoutledgeFarmer.

Grandin, T. (1996) *Thinking in Pictures and Other Reports from My Life with Autism*. Toronto: First Vintage Books.

Humphreys, T. (1996) *A Different Kind of Teacher*. Dublin: Gill and Macmillan.

—. (1998) *A Different Kind of Discipline*. Dublin: Gill and MacMillan.

Jensen, E. (2008) *Brain-based Learning*. Thousand Oaks, CA: Corwin Press.

Kaplan, L. J. (1984) *Adolescence: The Farewell to Childhood*. New York: Simon and Shuster.

Keddie, N. (1976) *Tinker, Taylor … the Myth of Cultural Deprivation*. Harmondsworth: Penguin.

Kohlberg, L. (1969) *States in the Development of Moral Thought and Action*. New York: Holt, Rhinehart and Winston.

Kutnik, P., and Jules, V. (1988) 'Pupils' perceptions of a good teacher: a developmental perspective from Trinidad and Tobago', Unpublished research, Sussex University.

Kyriacou, C. (2009) *Effective Teaching in Schools*. Cheltenham: Nelson Thornes.

Leask, M.Turner, T., and Coleman, J. (2005) 'Adolescence' in Moon, B., and S. Mayes (eds), *Teaching and Learning in a Secondary School*. Abingdon: RoutledgeFalmer.

Marland, M., and Rogers, R. (2004) *How to be a Successful Form Tutor*. London: Continuum.

Munn, P., and Lloyd, G. (2005) 'Exclusion and excluded pupils.' *British Educational Research Journal*, 31, (2), 205–21.

NASUWT (2010) 'Student behaviour'. www.nasuwt.org.uk/Informationand Advice/NASUWTPolicyStatements/OthercurrentPolicyStatements/index.htm [acccessed 24 December 2010].

NUT (2010) 'Student behaviour'. www.glosnut.co.uk/docs/behaviour.pdf Olsen, J., and Cooper, P. (2002) *Dealing with Disruptive Students in the Classroom*. London: Kogan Page (Times Educational Supplement).

Paxton, K., and Estay, I. (2007) *Counselling People on the Autistic Spectrum*. London: Jessica Kinglsey Publishers.

Phinn, G. (2001) *It Takes One to Know One*. London: Puffin.

QCAAW (2000) *Challenging Students: Enabling Access*. Cardiff: QCAAW.

Rist, R. (1970) 'Student social class and teacher expectations: the self-ful-filling prophecy in ghetto educations'. *Harvard Educational Review,* 40, 411–50.

Rogers, B. (2011) *You Know the Fair Rule.* London: Pitman.

Rutter, M. (1983) *A Measure of Our Values, Goals, and Dilemmas in the Upbringing of Children.* London: Pitman.

Schindler, J. (2010) *Transformative Classroom Management.* San Francisco: Jossey Bass Teacher.

Schön, D. (1983) *The Reflective Practitioner.* New York: Basic Books.

Shaw, S., and Hawes, T. (1998) *Effective Teaching and Learning in the Primary Classroom.* Leicester: Optimal Learning.

Startup, I. (2003) *Running Your Own Tutor Group.* London: Continuum.

Taylor, P. (1962) "Children's evaluations of the characteristics of a good teacher". *British Journal of Educational Psychology*, 32, 258–66.

Wragg, T. (1995) 'Teachers' first encounters with their classes' in Moon, B., and Shelton, A. (eds), *Teaching and Learning in the Secondary School.* London: Open University.

Zimpher, N., and Howey K. (1987) 'Adapting supervisory practices to dif-ferent orientations of teaching competence'. *Journal of Curriculum and Supervision*, Winter, 2, 104–7.

Index